Charming Your Way to the Top

MICHAEL LEVINE

Charming Your Way to the Top

HOLLYWOOD'S PREMIER P. R. EXECUTIVE

SHOWS YOU HOW TO GET AHEAD

THE LYONS PRESS

Guilford, Connecticut

An imprint of The Globe Pequot Press

The Lyons Press is an imprint of The Globe Pequot Press.

10 9 8 7 6 5 4 3 2 1

Printed in the United States of America
Book design and composition by Diane Gleba Hall

ISBN 1-59228-440-X

Library of Congress Cataloging-in-Publication Data is available on file.

*This book is dedicated with significant respect
to Jeff Cohen for both his loyalty
and extraordinary talent.*

Contents

Acknowledgments

I'm lucky. I get to say publicly to the special people in my life how much they mean to me. To each of them: my appreciation for their help with this book and, most of all, their unwavering friendship and love.

My literary agent, Craig Nelson.

My special friends, Peter Bart, Adam Christing, Richard Imprecia, John McKillop, Cable Neuhaus, Alyse Reynolds, and Lisa Yukelson.

Special thanks to Jeff Cohen for commitment to excellence in assisting with this book, and a special thank-you to Jay Cassell and Lisa Purcell from The Lyons Press.

To my staff, Clarissa Clarke, Liam Collopy, Shannon Hartigan, Jodi Jackson, Brian McWilliams, and Dawn Miller.

Interns interested in working in Mr. Levine's Los Angeles office should contact:

> Intern Coordinator, Levine Communications Office
> 1180 S. Beverly Drive, Los Angeles, CA 90035
> www.lcoonline.com
> e-mail: mlevine@lcoonline.com

Charm Isn't Lucky—It's Smart

Charm is good business.

That sentence might seem like the biggest "duh" you've ever heard, but it might actually be the understatement of the year. And nobody is paying attention. *Charm is good business.* It can significantly increase your income, improve your status, and establish and maintain your reputation. It can mean the difference, in some cases, between success and bankruptcy. That's how crucial the concept and practice of charm can be in business today.

What's most astounding is that the vast majority of business people don't automatically understand the concept of charm. You'd think it would be a reflex, a conditioned response in business to "turn on the charm" when dealing with customers, clients, associates, employees, competitors, or potential clients. And since the list of "potential clients" for many businesses can include Everybody, the idea that someone in any job, anywhere, *ever* is *not* making the maximum effort to be as charming as possible all the time is stupefying. How to Succeed in Business Without Really Trying? Try being charming.

This is not simply one man's opinion—it's clear through research studies, published articles and treatises, opinion polls, and just plain old real life that charm is extremely well valued in our society. People can say whatever they want about former President Bill Clinton's policies or his personal conduct, but no one who ever met the man has failed to comment on his personal charm. The same can be said for Ronald Reagan. And in this country, it's hard to get much farther in life than to be president of the United States. President Bush, too, can be considered charming, but in an entirely different way.

Charm is also evident in movie stars—when they want to show it. Interviews with stars are meant to convey their charm, so the public, which buys the tickets and ultimately pays the salaries, will feel that this person is "friendly" or that one is "down to earth." We will "like" them better, thus assuring performers solid, loyal fan bases that will keep them working for the foreseeable future. Charm pays.

It's not only true, however, for those in entertainment or politics. The surly garage owner will probably attract fewer customers than the one across the street who is well known for his concern and easy manner. Have you ever changed lanes at the supermarket because the "nice" cashier was working nearby and the "grumpy" one was at your lane? Have you ever chosen one dry cleaner over another? Was it because the level of cleaning was *really* all that noticeable or the prices *that* much lower, or was it because the second cleaner seemed "friendly?"

Charm draws customers.

By the same token, in industries that don't deal directly with the public, it's often the case that charm can propel a worker to a higher level of responsibility (and pay). Maybe the charming person who can't

do the job won't be promoted, but when two employees of equal com-
petence are in line for a promotion, do you think the one who practices
charm well is going to be at a *dis*advantage?

Charm gets noticed.

When a customer or client contacts a firm for the first time, walks
into a store for the first time, or encounters an employee for the first
time, charm—exercised properly and sincerely—creates an impression.
If you walk into an exclusive restaurant and the maître d' welcomes you
warmly, knows your name from the reservation and uses it, seats you
quickly and wishes you a pleasant dinner, will you notice? Wouldn't
you notice even if the counter help at the local McDonald's smiled and
welcomed you in some way other than to recite the corporate-dictated
slogan when you enter?

Charm creates an impression. Usually a good one.

When something in business goes wrong—the overnight package
doesn't arrive, the copying machine breaks down, the client doesn't receive the proposal when it's expected—is it better to become defensive
and blame others for what went wrong, or to apologize, explain the
problem, and promise that no such thing will ever happen again? Which
way is more charming? Which way will keep the client on your roster?

Charm soothes and heals.

If you have competition (and who doesn't?), the ability to be
charming, congenial, and considerate will help your business not only
to stand out, but also to distance itself from its competition. It can
become part of your brand: the charming bookstore, the charming
insurance company, the charming computer solutions provider.

Charm can identify.

Does all this mean that a person in business needs only to be
charming in order to succeed? Of course not. Above all, a business
must deliver what it promises, and no amount of congeniality can

replace that. The most charming man in the world (and we'll meet him later) can run a business into the ground if he doesn't successfully deliver the basic needs pledged to his customers.

But it's important to note that, quite often, business decisions are made based on subjective criteria. If two businesses can provide a certain product, and provide it for roughly the same price, the customer will have to choose between the two based on other variables. These may include geographical location, speed of delivery, or some other intangible.

The deal could very well depend on the ability of one business-person to charm another.

Don't discount that idea. It's not simply a question of being able to project an image of friendliness, or even courtesy, something else that is severely lacking in today's business climate. Charm is not false, and it can't be "put on." It can be learned, but it can't be faked. When you, as a business owner, employer, employee, or representative, meet with a potential or current customer (client), you have two options: you can be curt, arrogant, and impatient, or you can be charming. Even on days when it doesn't come naturally, "charming" is the better choice, in every case.

That's what this book is all about. The concept of charm may seem antiquated or anachronistic in today's cold, bottom-line business world, but it is the polar opposite of those things. Charm is as important to business today as a cell phone and a briefcase, and in some businesses, more so. It is an attribute that can truly make the difference between success and failure, and does so on a startlingly regular basis.

Charm is often confused with *courtesy*, and while that is a natural mistake to make, it is still a mistake. Courtesy is behavior dictated by certain rules, like etiquette, and those who are courteous generally act within those rules. Courtesy doesn't necessarily imply creativity, nor does it mean that one is "going the extra mile." It means, simply, that the rules of civil behavior, in business or otherwise, are being met, not necessarily exceeded.

Charm, on the other hand, is a concept that is the very definition of exceeding expectations. In a civilization as coarse and crude as the one we now inhabit, it is easy to mistake courtesy for charm, because so few people are courteous to begin with. But the person who goes farther, who looks for ways to be courteous beyond what the "rule book" may dictate, is on the road to being thought of as charming. And that is very much the subject of this book.

Why Charming? ——

In 1961, a department store executive attended a lunchtime concert given by a local band that hadn't made much of a name for itself outside a radius of a few city blocks. He listened to the half hour or so of music, wasn't terribly impressed, given the dreadful acoustics of the place and the band's lackadaisical attitude toward the gig. It wasn't until he met the musicians afterward that they made any kind of impression upon him.

"I was struck, mostly, by their personal charm," Brian Epstein would later relate in an interview. Not long after, he signed the first contract to manage the Beatles, based on exactly that attribute.

In the world of Hollywood public relations and publicity, where I work, charm is a constant—personality is both an attribute and a commodity in show business—but not everyone is charming. The smart ones are, and the successful ones often are. I've worked with personalities as varied as Barbra Streisand, Michael Jackson, Vanna White, and Mary Hart, among many others. And I can tell you from first-person experience, charm is a major attribute of everyone who is successful in Hollywood.

Does that mean that everyone in show business behaves beautifully and courteously all the time? Absolutely not! I've been privy to tantrums and meltdowns far beyond what the average businessperson has to contend with on a daily basis. I've thrown a few myself, to tell the truth. But I have taught myself how to be charming, and I believe that those at the top of any business—not only the entertainment industry—must do exactly that, too.

Can charm be taught? Certainly it can. I do not believe that charm is necessarily an inborn trait. Of course some people find it more easily than others, but that doesn't mean we can't *teach* ourselves how to find the charm that lies within. We can study others, assess ourselves, and make the kind of determinations all people in business must make when they are honestly trying to reach the pinnacle of their professions.

You can, indeed, charm your way to the top. It is my belief, in fact, that without charm you can't make it to the top at all. You might be able to reach a certain level of responsibility and success, but in order to be the very best in any profession, in order to find yourself at the top of the food chain in your industry, looking down on all others, some measure of charm is an *absolute necessity*. Note that I did not, in that sentence, use the words "helpful attribute" or "major plus." I said, "absolute necessity." And I couldn't possibly stress that idea more strongly.

I know show business executives who think they are above the concept of charm. They don't need charm, they believe, because they have ability and contacts. So they don't make phone calls themselves to confirm a business meeting. They don't send gifts or thank-you notes after a successful deal is completed. They don't feel it's necessary to take a moment to compliment a coworker or employee on a job well done.

None of these people are at the highest levels of their industries, I should note. Not one. The ones at the top have charm. It flows from the top. Those with Ivy League degrees and cutthroat attitudes, but absolutely no ability to be charming, are usually stuck in the middle of the pack somewhere. Sometimes, they don't even make it that high.

This book isn't designed to convince you that charm is a valuable tool to possess in business. The fact is, if you're striving for the heights of success, charm is a *necessity* in business. This book is meant to be a guide, a road map through the dark, winding path that is the way to success. It strives to explain not just *why* charm is important, but *how* it is important, and more important, how to develop the kind of charm you need to rise to the very top of your industry.

Charm *can* be taught.

I am living proof. Charm does not come particularly easily to me. When I decided I wanted to start my own Hollywood public relations firm, I realized that I'd need as much charm as I could muster, and that posed a problem. For someone whose first impulse is not necessarily the charming one, my being in a field such as public relations, which depends so heavily on personality and the ability to talk to people, was not a simple choice. It would require a good deal of self-training and learned behavior.

So that is exactly what I managed to do. I observed other people, which is the best possible way to assess one's own behavior. I compared my reactions to those I saw around me. I chose role models whom I thought exuded the kind of charm I wished myself to have, and I analyzed what made them especially personable. And I took special note of people I thought were unusually *not* charming. What were they doing wrong? Which points did they ignore? And how, in my opinion, could they improve their behavior and further their goals?

Today, while I hardly consider myself in the Charm Hall of Fame, I know how to wield charm as a tool, and a weapon when necessary. I understand its power and can exercise it when I think it's important to do so. I know what it is to be charming, even if I believe it does not come to me naturally.

And as a result, my business has flourished. I have represented such respected Hollywood luminaries as Sandra Bullock, Cameron Diaz, Prince, David Bowie, Michael J. Fox, Fleetwood Mac, Charlton Heston, Linda Evans, Robert Evans, Demi Moore, and Ozzy Osbourne, as well as corporate clients such as Pizza Hut and others. I have never worked a day in my life for an employer who was not myself. And my business is considered among the top publicity and public relations firms in Los Angeles.

I don't say that to impress you or to brag about some of my professional accomplishments—I list these things because I want you to know that I have *learned* charm. None of my success would have been possible had I not taught myself what I believe to be the power and the use of charm in business, and it certainly would not have happened if I hadn't paid any attention to charm overall. I reaped the rewards because I took the time to teach myself how to be charming, and I believe I can do the same for you, if you meet me halfway.

First, you have to have some natural ability—not to be charming, but to have a talent that is marketable in your business. Charm will take you far, but it will not hand you a career all by itself. There is no job description for "charming person," although many have tried to get by strictly on this one attribute and nothing else. They have failed. So, you need to be doing your job the best way you know how—with or without utilizing charm.

Next, you have to be willing to try. No one can *force* you to be charming, or trick you into doing something considerate and helpful. You have to have the desire on your own. I'm willing to bet that you do, since you've already picked up this book and read this far. So, you're already part of the way to success.

But you have work to do. You have to *observe* charm in others and *analyze* what it does and how it is done. I will guide you through the process each step of the way, making sure you understand and master each piece of the puzzle before we put it all together to help you get to the pinnacle of your business, as far as you can go.

We'll examine some of the ways famous people—in the entertainment industry and other fields—use charm, examine the ones who don't and how it affects their careers, and see if we can extend the techniques of the most charming people in the world to your goals. As I did when I began, we will learn by example.

Also, we can start by determining how charm has become such a precious commodity. Those things that are rarest, don't forget, are most valuable—nobody would care about diamonds or gold if they were easily found in everyone's backyard. So it is with charm—the less we see of it, the more valuable and important it seems to become.

But we'll have to focus on the way charm can be used *in business*, which is something no one has ever examined before. Charm simply isn't considered a "serious" business attribute, despite its almost central importance to most people striving for success. So we will make sure to examine business-related examples, and discuss charm and its importance to CEOs and company owners. You'll see through their stories and reactions the vital role charm plays in business situations (chiefly meetings and negotiations, but also so much more).

We'll meet the Most Charming Man Ever and discover the secrets it took for him to become that, but we will also visit with his polar opposite, in which we'll discover the dark side of charm—how it can destroy as well as nurture.

There will be discussions of telephone charm and charm on the Internet (if such a thing is possible—and it is!). I'll tell you some stories about people I've worked with who both did and did not use charm successfully, and if I can bring myself to do so, I'll tell you stories about how I might have slipped and done a few things that weren't exactly Fred Astaire material myself.

Along the way, please pay attention to the habits and learned behaviors of all the people we meet. In fact, pay attention to *all* the people you meet during your daily life, since they will all be role models for the "Do" and "Don't" categories of charm. Yes, emulate the ones you think are especially successful, and no, definitely don't copy the people who are regularly rude or discourteous.

Being charming doesn't mean you always have to behave like someone bound by a strict code of ethics; it doesn't mean you have to follow every rule blindly and unthinkingly. Quite the opposite is true. The real power of charm comes with *creativity*, and that is only possible when a person is free to try new things and, overall, to be oneself. There is no point to being charming if you're behaving like an automaton.

The key rule is: have fun with it. Be yourself, but better. Do unto others the way you would have them do unto you. And, while you're doing all that:

Charm your way to the top.

> Michael Levine
> Los Angeles, California
> www.lcoonline.com

Charming Your Way to the Top

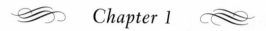

Chapter 1

How Things Got This Way

In the beginning, humans were not charming.

Things were simpler for our ancestors millions of years ago. The biggest, strongest man got to lead the group. He did so until a bigger, stronger man (or perhaps an animal or act of nature) showed him who was boss, and then the tribe followed *that* leader.

Charm did not play a very large role in that arrangement. But times have changed (thank goodness) since the days of those primitive humans, and these days, charm can play a tremendous role in a leader's ascension to power, either in politics or business.

The problem is, we haven't changed all that much since our cave days. We have, in fact, regressed from a point we had reached not all that long ago, to a level where our society is as crude, coarse, and inconsiderate as in those days.

In fact, maybe these days are worse. After all, those first people didn't really expect any more than they got.

Charm has become a rare commodity, and that makes it something that is by definition very valuable. But that's not necessarily good news. It means we live in a society that's so decidedly rude, someone who exhibits charm at any level is considered an uncommon and amazing specimen. We have not evolved all that much in terms of our manners or our *desire* to charm others. We have the ability, but we never seem to use it.

In modern society, walking into a supermarket, a fast-food restaurant, or a video rental store can be an exercise in rudeness. The workers manning the store—including many managers—are, at best, indifferent to customers and their needs, and are too often downright hostile when asked a question or required to do the job for which they are being paid. Everyone has a "bad service" story, and when it is told, listeners in the room all nod their heads in recognition: "Yes, they've heard *that* one before."

The problem isn't that there are a few places where workers aren't charming anymore. The problem is that this has become the *norm*, the accepted level of overall service that customers assume will be in use when they enter a retail establishment, unless it is an especially expensive and exclusive one. In those cases, snootiness takes over for apathy, and customers seen as less than affluent and upscale are treated as if they've walked into the wrong bar.

No matter how you look at it, charm is definitely missing from these scenarios. And there's no reason for that to be. It's just as easy to perform a task with, at least, courtesy for the client, as it is to perform the same task and be rude at the same time.

A person who walks into Burger King (or, to be fair, *any* fast-food restaurant) expecting the welcoming, smiling help featured in the chain's advertising campaigns is most likely in for a very rude awakening, "rude" being the key word in that phrase. More often than not, the best one can expect is a curt welcome that sounds like it's being read off a card, food that arrives in a bag and is often not all that similar to the order that was placed, and facilities in the location that are, let's say, not so clean you can eat off them.

And we have come to accept—even to expect—that kind of service. That's the scary part.

Charm in the counter help would make things work differently. It would cost not a cent more, take not a minute longer, cut into revenues by zero percent, and change the well-regulated system of food preparation not a bit. It can be taught as part of the general training each employee receives, and it would cost the company nothing. So, why are corporations *not* teaching charm to their employees on any level, anywhere?

Because it's not a priority. Customers don't expect it, and executives think it won't increase profits in any way. But there is a growing mountain of evidence to suggest that assumption is not in the least true.

Customer satisfaction surveys are showing that consumers are less and less satisfied with the level of service they receive generally, and they are complaining ever more loudly about companies that have traditionally prided themselves on fast service, such as McDonald's and other fast-food restaurants.

Such companies have seen their sales erode, and there's no reason to believe that customer service didn't contribute to those declines. In fact, if the surveys are to be believed (and I think they are), service is a major contributor to the lower revenues being totaled by many service-oriented businesses.

Would a little charm hurt so much?

The real question is: How did things deteriorate to this level?

How did a society that at one time boasted courteous service and a degree of charm from its workers in service industries such as food and gasoline erode to the point that customers not only accept a listless, even hostile, approach, but they also *assume* they will get exactly that?

To chronicle the decline of charm in American society, we first must define what we mean by "charm." Many people confuse charm with *politeness* or *courtesy*, and while it is a natural mistake to make, neither of those qualities—each of which is *included* in charm—defines "charm."

Charm is the difference between a rote recitation of "God bless you" when someone sneezes, and a genuine interest in the person's health. It is *not* "Wow, your rack looks great in that dress, Sally," and *is* "That's a really nice color for you, Monica." When a person says "thank you" for a gift, that's courtesy. When he sends a thank-you *note*, that's charm.

Therefore, charm is going the extra mile, while courtesy is the act of not doing something offensive. Charm is all about the other person, and courtesy is about you. Charm is about respect; courtesy is about following rules.

A working definition of charm, for our purposes, is: *charm is the art of making the other person believe you care.*

Certainly, that's an oversimplification, but it suits our purposes nicely. People believe that to be charming, one must have a great wit, physical grace, creative talent, or a really smooth line of talk. While none of those things hurts, they are not essential to charm. The only thing that *is* essential is that you *make the other person believe you care.*

The easiest way to do this, of course, is to care. That is efficient, profitable, and has the added benefit of being the right thing to do. In retail businesses, the other person is the customer, and all she or he really wants you to care about is getting your job done properly. This can be done in two ways, and I'll leave it to you to decide which one is more charming:

```
INT. FAST-FOOD RESTAURANT - AFTERNOON
CUSTOMER enters from street. The CLERK behind
the counter yawns as he approaches, and speaks
in a monotone:

CLERK
Welcome to (fill in name of fast-food place). Can
I help you?

CUSTOMER
Yes, thank you. May I have a burger with no pickles,
please?

[The Clerk barely manages to disguise his amusement.]

CLERK
If you really want to, but it'll take at least
twelve minutes.

CUSTOMER
Twelve minutes? Isn't that a long time?

[Clerk, talking to his girlfriend on the side,
doesn't answer.]

CLERK
You want the burger, or not?

CUSTOMER
Yeah, okay. No pickles.

CLERK
Right. Stand to the side. I've got people waiting in
line.
```

Here's the second scenario (and don't tell me it's not possible):

```
The CUSTOMER enters from the street. As he
approaches the counter, he notices the CLERK's
friendly smile. The Clerk speaks in an attentive,
yet conversational, tone.
```

CLERK
Good afternoon, Sir. Welcome to (fill in name of
fast-food place)! How may I help you today?

CUSTOMER
Well, hello. Would it be possible to get a burger
with no pickles?

CLERK
(looking a little disappointed) I'm so sorry, Sir,
but our system is set up in such a way that special
orders take extra time. It could be twelve minutes
before I can get that for you.

CUSTOMER
Twelve minutes, huh? That is a while.

CLERK
I know. If you'd like to speak to the manager about
it, I'm sure he'll be happy to . . .

CUSTOMER
Oh no, that's not necessary. It's all right; I'm not
in that big a hurry. I'll take the burger, with no
pickles, please.

[The clerk has never left the counter during the
conversation. He punches in the order, and looks
up again, smiles.]

CLERK
Thank you for the order, Sir. Is there anything else
I can get you with that?

CUSTOMER
Yes, a large fries and a soda.

CLERK
Terrific. I'll tell you what. Since you have to wait
for your burger, the soda is on the house.

CUSTOMER
Why, thank you!

CLERK
And if you'll just wait at your table, I'll be glad
to bring you your order when it's ready.

CUSTOMER
Thanks again.

There's no point in even asking which scenario better fits the definition of "charming" that we established above. By making the customer know that he cares about his performance—which means not just that he does his job well, but that it means a good deal to him that it is done right—the clerk in the second scene proves to the customer that the customer's needs are important. He, the clerk, *cares* about the customer, understands his concerns, and works hard to meet them. The clerk is smiling and attentive, listens to the customer at all times, and seems to care about the inconvenience he encounters. When an obstacle to fulfilling the customer's needs—the extra time for the burger—is established, the clerk offers an apology for the system and the inconvenience built into it. He also asks if the customer wants to complain to a superior, and when the customer agrees to endure the inconvenience, makes an offer of a free drink to compensate. The customer here is more likely to walk away with a positive feeling about the fast-food chain than the one in the first scenario.

And what's interesting? The customer in the second scene didn't have fewer problems than the one in the first. Being charming didn't change the way the burger place cooks its food, so the clerk's attitude couldn't make the special order happen faster. Because the clerk *did* care, or at least gave the impression of caring, the second customer understood that there was no better way for the clerk to handle the situation, that he couldn't speed up the process, and that it wasn't his fault. Where the clerk in the first scenario should be immediately placed on probation for his attitude, the clerk in the second scene is more likely to be promoted sometime soon, because he can handle potential problems and make the customer appreciate his visit there— to the point that the customer might actually recommend this fast-food outlet to others. That is the power of what charm can do.

How did it work? It worked because the clerk made sure the customer understood that he cared. That can be extrapolated to *any* business, and virtually *any* circumstance. It won't always have exactly the same happy ending as our scenario above, but charm will *never* make a situation worse, and will very often improve it.

Because our society has deteriorated so far, because charm is such a rarely seen commodity, it is a more noticeable, more desirable, more valuable property than ever before. It is as useful a tool and as devastating a weapon as anything in the business arsenal, an implement capable of catching your competition off balance and elevating your own performance and results immeasurably. And the cost of using it? Absolutely nothing, unless you count the price of this book.

Consider your own dealings with retail chains, other businesses, civil employees, or virtually everyone in the course of performing the tasks that make up their jobs. Isn't it much more likely that you'll find sullen, apathetic, irritated, and surly people just "putting in their time" until being released to go home? Doesn't that happen to you much more frequently than finding pleasant, interested, genuinely concerned employees trying their absolute best to fulfill the mission you've assigned them (either directly, as an employer, or indirectly, as a client or customer)?

Now. Which ones do you remember more fondly? Which ones do you remember better? For that matter, which ones do you *remember*?

See my point? Charm is not only useful and valuable, it is also *memorable*. And in business, there is almost nothing better than being remembered. In fact, the only thing better than being remembered is being remembered *fondly*. And that is what charm can do for you.

If you had the experience detailed above, in which the fast-food customer was ignored and diminished by the counter help, would you remember it? Perhaps you would. But would you remember it *fondly*? I tend to doubt it.

But, if you had the second experience, in which the drink is on the house and the counter help made sure you got the order you wanted, with the smallest delay possible under the circumstances, would you remember *that*? I'll bet you would, and you would also remember it fondly. Would you even *consider* going back to the first fast-food restaurant? Would you even consider *not* patronizing the second one on a regular basis?

Charm is a huge advantage in business, and the good news is that now, with a population made complacent by years of bad, completely non-charming service at virtually every turn, the charming businessperson will be that much more noticeable. It is that much easier to become charming, and that much more of an advantage to display it.

Wait, it gets better. With customer satisfaction ratings going down on an annual basis, it's clear that people expect less and less to find a charming employee behind the counter, on the phone, or in the street. It is, therefore, now easier to stand out than it has ever been before. Keep reading, and you'll see how to become more charming. It's so easy, it's almost embarrassing. Really.

Chapter 2

Charm Is the Missing Link

Because charm is, as we've demonstrated, so vitally important to success in business, you'd assume that it would be practiced so commonly and so carefully that we'd all expect it in every aspect of our business lives. After all, something that can make such an enormous difference in business would surely be a priority for every business owner, executive, and employee, right?

Amazingly, no. As any of us who deals with retail or service clerks on a regular basis can attest, charm is so underutilized it's practically vanished from the business map.

How can this be? After all, if you're in the least bit logical, you have to admit that using a tool that can improve your reputation, advance your agenda, and further your chances for success in *any* business, all at a cost of *nothing*, should be second nature. We should all be charming to each other at all times, just out of enlightened self-interest, because at some point, that charm could come back to reward us for our efforts and help us achieve our goals.

But this is quite obviously not the case in our society, which becomes cruder and coarser every day. It is certainly not the rule in business, where we are treated with indifference when we're lucky enough to reach *that* level, and with disrespect reaching the level of disdain when we're not.

Charm, you see, is the missing link in business. It can build a bridge between you and your goals, between advancement and stagnation, between you and your colleagues or employees. It can forge bonds between your business and its clientele that would not be possible otherwise. But it is so infrequently noticeable in our current society that it might just as well be kept in a museum.

Imagine a trip to the Charm Museum, where courteous guides usher you into rooms depicting acts of charm and courtesy no longer practiced in modern business. In one wing, thank-you notes from famous executives that furthered their relationships with clients or allies. In another, recorded instances of compliments paid to coworkers. And a whole floor could be devoted to retail employees who made an extra effort, if enough examples could be found to fill that much space.

I think people would flock to such a building, to relive the nostalgic rush of a bygone age, when it was possible to *expect* charming behavior from those you encountered in the course of a typical day. I believe people are so hungry for a taste of charm that they'd pay for the opportunity to see it up close. If it were actually available to them in everyday life, do you think charm could make a difference in people's buying habits or decision making?

The problem is that most people have become so conditioned to surly service, apathetic attitudes, and cutthroat competition that it never occurs to them things could be different. And that's why the link of charm is missing from American—and for a large part, global—business today.

In order to reinstate the missing link, it will be necessary for you to remember the Golden Rule of Charm in Business: *always* make the other person think you care about *him (or her)*. This is a variation on our general definition of charm, but it is a directive—something that commands attention and instructs specifically on a tactic to use in your day-to-day business life, and your personal life as well.

Always make the other person think you care about him.

Even better: always make the other person *know* you care.

Charm isn't something you can fake, but it is something you can learn through practice. If you can do enough to convince other people —clients, superiors, coworkers, employees, customers, everyone— that you really and truly care about their concerns, their priorities, that you are willing to help solve their problems, you will be exhibiting the purest form of charm, and you will indeed find yourself at the top when the day is done. People respond to the missing link because they consider it a wonderful novelty.

Here's a quick example. I've been in business in Hollywood for more than twenty years, and I'd estimate that I go to business lunches nearly every day. Half the time I'll pay the bill for the person I'm meeting at lunch, and half the time, I'll be treated by that person.

No matter how many times we've been to lunch, I will *always* make sure I send a thank-you note later that day or the following day. Every time, without fail. That is, I'm willing to admit, an obvious attempt on my part to be charming in business. But here's the interesting fact. In more than twenty years in Hollywood, meeting executives, movie stars, directors, musicians, businesspeople and countless others, *I have never received a single thank-you note for a lunch I bought.* Not just a low percentage—*not one* of the people I've met for business lunches has ever formally thanked me for buying a meal, which can sometimes be quite expensive (as are the ones I thank them for, I want to point out). And they say there's no such thing as a free lunch.

Now, I'm sure a good number of the people who read this book will react with no surprise at all. "Of *course* no one ever sent a thank-you note for lunch! Who sends thank-you notes anymore, anyway? It was *business*." And rather than wondering why the other people I mention aren't trying to charm me, many—if not most—readers will wonder why I would go to all that trouble to try and be charming to *them*.

And in that reaction—in the incredulity about my seemingly over-the-top, inexplicable behavior—lies my point. People don't expect you to be charming. In fact, if you're merely civil, most will find that a refreshing change of pace. But when you go out of your way, when you make the extra effort, and especially when you make an unexpected gesture that shows you're thinking about someone else's needs, you are making an impression. You are creating a positive memory of yourself that can translate into a business decision in the future. You are creating an opportunity for yourself.

In short, you are charming your way to the top.

I know that in my everyday travels, if a sales clerk, a cab driver, or an executive assistant goes out of his way to look out for my welfare, I will remember it. I'll notice when I'm visiting someone's office and I'm offered a soft drink or water. I'll notice when the counter help at a fast-food restaurant even smiles or says "thank you." I'll notice when an invitation to a press event I'm promoting is accepted—or rejected—by the addressee, rather than an assistant.

I'll make a note of these things, maybe not on paper, but mentally. I'll make sure I remember which people did the extra things that make my day just a little bit easier or more pleasant. And I will more than likely go out of my way to see that person and do the same for her—perhaps by giving her my business, or doing a favor when I can, without being asked. If I am charmed, I will make an effort to be that much more charming in the future.

The missing link, you see, can bridge very different worlds, and it can create alliances where none existed before.

Charm can, in fact, get you started in a career or a business. There's no disputing its overwhelming value in job interviews, and those starting their own businesses will attest to the golden sheen charm can place on a first sales call or client meeting.

Carole V. Bartholomeaux, president of BARTHOLOMEAUX/Public Relations, LLC, in Phoenix, Arizona, recalls applying for a job as a cocktail waitress when she was, as she puts it, "a starving college student." She says she didn't get the job, but her attention to detail and the ability to make the manager think she cared—her charm—helped improve the situation considerably.

"I was the only applicant who came to the interview in a dress and jacket rather than cut-offs or tank tops, and I got a personal interview with the manager," Bartholomeaux recalls. "Since Mother would never let me play with my toys the day after Christmas until all my thank-you notes were written, I, of course, wrote the manager a thank-you.

"Two days later, he called and said, 'We have been thinking of hiring a woman as a part-time manager/bouncer. I have never received a thank-you note for a job interview before. If you want it, the job is yours.'"

That was the beginning of a successful career, and even if the job was a part-time manager at a chain restaurant, it was still important to Bartholomeaux, and started her on a road that has become more and more successful as she has traveled it.

It was the "missing link" aspect of the story that had the deepest impact, however. It wasn't just that Bartholomeaux wrote and sent a thank-you note for a job interview—it was that she was the *only* applicant to do so, and to dress for the interview as she would for work. That made an impression, and the impression made the difference. Even though she did not get the first position she applied for, Bartholomeaux was offered the second job, which held more responsibility and received higher pay.

That example, simple though it may have been, can be repeated over and over again in all business applications. Every CEO had to get a first job. Every entrepreneur had to make a first sale. Every superstar entertainer had to get that first gig. But it doesn't end there, either.

As each climbed the ladder, there were rungs that couldn't be reached without a display of charm. The ultrasuccessful in our society, even if they seem to be difficult and demanding once they've achieved the highest levels of their professions, must have been charming and considerate at *some* level to get noticed, and promoted.

Charm, remember, does not mean being nice to everybody. It does not mean acting subservient or being a doormat for everyone you encounter. Charm means *making the other person believe you care*. There are many examples of those who are not witty, compassionate, or even polite, but can be considered, under the right circumstances, charming. And quite often, that has to do with the *context* in which one is placed. The "missing link" theory enters into this discussion frequently.

Think, for example, of the Hannibal Lecter character from the novel and film *The Silence of the Lambs*. This sociopathic killer—a man so dangerous he had to be bound to a handcar and put in a hockey mask whenever he was transported out of his prison cell—was able to convince people to do his bidding even when it would cause them great physical pain. He was able to get FBI agents to act against rules laid out for them by superiors. Perhaps most significantly, despite his tendencies toward extreme violence and antisocial behavior, the character, as portrayed by Anthony Hopkins on-screen, was able to convince audiences to *root* for him, no matter how frightening and dangerous a man he most certainly was.

How? Hannibal Lecter, when he wanted to be, was *charming*. He was erudite and witty, spoke with a great deal of intelligence and logic, and made the other characters believe he cared about their concerns.

Remember, the Jodie Foster character, Special Agent Clarice Starling, was sent by a superior officer to interview Lecter in the hope that he would *help* in the investigation into another serial killer. And in the end, he did provide the information necessary to apprehend the other man.

By that time, Lecter had escaped his prison, and in a horrifying scene of violence, had killed the two guards assigned to him. And even so, audiences found the character charming, and demanded more of him, finally flocking to two other films in which Hopkins portrayed the mad psychiatrist.

What does Hannibal Lecter prove? Certainly, as a fictional character, he can have any attributes the author of the novel decided to imbue upon him. Lecter could have been a wild-eyed, drooling madman who frightened everyone he met. He could have been seen as someone who hated other people and would take any opportunity to destroy them. But instead, Lecter was given the power to charm. Why? Because it was plausible—the man was a psychiatrist who needed patients, he was a killer who needed to know his victims, and he was an inmate who wanted to get out of jail. Charm helps in all these pursuits.

I'm not suggesting, of course, that charm makes a good serial killer, nor that this is a goal you should pursue. Hannibal Lecter is a fictional character. But think about how such a negative person, someone with that many extremely unattractive traits, could be made sympathetic, someone an audience would actually want to see more of? Only charm can do that.

In more admirable pursuits, like those in the business world, charm can do more. We'll assume that you are *not* a homicidal maniac, and therefore don't need to redeem your personality to everyone you meet. Let's assume, rather, that you are in business, and want to advance. You have far fewer negative traits to overcome, so you're already at an advantage. And since you probably aren't going to threaten anyone physically today, you can concentrate instead on how to make the right impression to get you closer to what your eventual goal is going to be.

Charm, the missing link, can do that for you.

You have another advantage, now. You have read enough of this book that you realize the value of charm, and can identify it when you see it. You can certainly define the quality of charm, and you know exactly how it can help you gain the edge you need to continue up the ladder you've started to climb. What you need now is further background in how to make charm work for you.

The first step is to make an *impression*, and charm is definitely a component in doing that the right way the first time.

$\iff$ *Chapter 3* $\iff$

Standing Out

It's common sense to say that before you can be a success in any business, you have to be *noticed*. After all, no business has ever attracted clients or customers, risen in reputation, or outperformed its competition by doing its best to remain anonymous.

These days, in fact, being noticed, and being noticed quickly, can be more important than any other factor in launching a new business or expanding an existing company. It is the difference between being accepted and being forgotten. Keep in mind that during the 2003 California gubernatorial recall election, it did not hurt Arnold Schwarzenegger to have name recognition.

But before he could be recognized, Schwarzenegger had to be *charming*. He made the people who knew his name believe that he cared about them, the ultimate job for a political candidate. And he did it in a remarkably short period of time, in a new area of achievement for him. How? Well, it didn't hurt that Arnold was internationally famous, of course, but it also was true that he managed to convey a message of caring and confidence. Charm.

Consider that this man's entire career could be considered a triumph of charm. Entering the Hollywood arena—one that I know well is as competitive and cutthroat as any on earth—armed with a muscular body and a thick Austrian accent, but plenty of ambition and a good deal of charm, Schwarzenegger has been beating the odds against him for a quarter century. He became a beloved action hero and actually branched into comedy successfully, playing against his own image, all the while looking for the next enterprise, the next challenge, the next obstacle.

And through it all, the smile never left his face and he never conveyed anything on screen other than charm, even when playing a villainous robot in the first *Terminator* film.

How does fictional charm, like that conveyed on-screen by Schwarzenegger, translate into real-life charm, which the voters clearly believed he possessed as well? By carefully cultivating his offscreen image to reflect the on-screen characters he played, the actor-turned-politician gave his fans what they wanted—a huge, strong hero who could also be seen as the guy next door. He made sure that some of the roles he played on-screen were meant to be "regular guys," and when he played a secret agent in *True Lies*, the joke was that he was such a nebbish that no one—not even his wife—would believe he could be a dashing spy.

But first, Arnold had to get noticed, and that's what he did in *Pumping Iron*, a 1977 documentary revolving around the Mr. Universe bodybuilding competition. Schwarzenegger doesn't come across as terribly charming, it should be noted (he makes some comments about how easy it is to deceive his opponents with bogus advice), but he makes an impression. He does have what used to be called *charisma,* and it is hard not to watch him when he's on-screen. But even if the false charm he so obviously used was transparent, it was also effective, and it taught Schwarzenegger lessons that would serve him well.

When he moved into action films, Schwarzenegger made sure to do as much publicity as possible, so that no matter how brutal the character he played on-screen would be, the audience could also see that the actor who played him was smiling, friendly, and—dare we say it?—charming. Movie fans who might not have seen (in fact, probably did not see) *Pumping Iron* would be introduced to this unlikely action star and see both images—the one written by a screenwriter, and the one cultivated by the actor himself during interviews and appearances.

Those getting their first look at Schwarzenegger in *Conan the Barbarian* or *The Terminator* would probably not consider him warm and fuzzy or the kind of guy they could sit down and have a beer with after work. But the man who showed up on *Entertainment Tonight* or *The Today Show* certainly was. He was accessible, he studied hard to minimize the accent, he spoke in general terms about his life as if it were the same as that of his audience.

Charm isn't the kind of thing that a person in the public eye can turn on and off, although it might seem that way sometimes. With the constant scrutiny by the media and the 24/7 level of reporting on anything a celebrity might do, being caught off-guard at any time can be disastrous. Even Schwarzenegger found that to be true during his brief gubernatorial campaign, as allegations of improper treatment of women and quotes from old interviews came back to haunt him.

How to handle that type of crisis? With charm, of course. Arnold immediately addressed charges against him, denied the false ones, and apologized for those with greater validity. He minimized their importance and they did not seem to hurt him in the polls. The first impression he had made decades earlier was serving him well.

"Hello, My Name Is . . ."

There are so many clichés about first impressions that saying anything about them at all seems to fall into the realm of redundancy. But it has to be noted that some things become clichés because they have so much truth in them that they are repeated ad infinitum. And the fact is that there's no second chance to make a first impression, and that first impressions do last a lifetime.

Consider how many people you meet in the course of an average day: in the elevator, on the bus, on the street, in the building where you work, the restaurant where you have lunch, the supermarket where you buy dinner. There are some you've seen dozens of times but you've never really noticed: the attendant at the gas station, the counter help at Burger King, the toll collector on the highway. You might have come into contact with these people hundreds of times, but they haven't made that *first impression* everyone's always talking about. Why? *Because they have not done anything that affected you either positively or negatively for you to remember.* They have simply fulfilled a role in your day, often without speaking at all.

Now, suppose one of those people had taken the time to greet you with a friendly smile and a kind word, had asked your name, or had made that moment in your life somehow easier or more enjoyable. You'd remember that, wouldn't you? By the same token, if one of them had been wearing a T-shirt bearing an offensive slogan, had used inappropriate language around you or your children, or had (through indifference or ineptitude) made that moment of your life more difficult or unpleasant, you'd remember *that*, too, wouldn't you?

Such a moment can make a first impression, either positive or negative, and here's the really tricky part of that equation—you *never know when it's coming.* You can't rehearse a first impression or study how to make it properly unless you are aware that such an event can come at any moment, under any circumstance, and with someone whom you have (obviously) never met. It's not often you can know ahead of time when such a meeting will take place.

So clearly, preparation for first impressions—and the necessity of charm in such circumstances can't possibly be overstated—has to involve forethought and practice. It is the kind of thing that can become second nature if enough attention and care are applied.

The most obvious way to ingratiate yourself to other people is to demonstrate interest in *them*. Women often complain that first dates are awful because the men they date rarely want to talk about anything but themselves. *Listening* as well as talking is a severely under-practiced skill and one that needs to be cultivated and used intelligently. It is simple and basic, but it is also true—we want people to listen to us.

This is not to say that divulging no information about yourself should be confused with charm. People do want to find out about you when they meet you, but they also want some indication that you respect their individuality, and are sincerely interested in what they have to say. Nothing could be simpler, and nothing could be more important.

Begin with a *name*. People like to feel that you are concerned enough to learn their names. Sure, it sounds ridiculously simple, but it is effective. A good trick for those with bad memories is to repeat a person's name back to him when you're introduced, and try to store that sound in your memory. Why do you think waiters at every restaurant you go to tell you their names before they take your order? Because they've been taught to do so, of course, but also because they want you to see them as something more than the function they serve—if you see Bill, and not The Waiter, you are likely to leave a more generous tip.

Once you learn the name, it is important to *use* it. Repeat it a couple of times in the course of your first conversation, to help you remember it, and to let the other person know you've made the effort to do so, and that you care about who he is. Phone messages left after business or personal meetings, after all, are more likely to be noticed if they contain the name of the person for whom the message is being left. But more about that later.

It's important, too, to notice something that makes a person who is new to you distinctive. After all, even your best friend was once a stranger, and you had to find something about her that made her stand out. In the beginning, it might have been a physical feature you remembered. She was the tall one, the redhead, the one with a dimple. But as you got to know her, her personality took over and that became more memorable and more distinctive than anything you noticed on a first glance.

We make the same judgments about celebrities. The first time you saw Bruce Willis on *Moonlighting*, was it the way he looked or the way he acted that commanded your attention? I'm willing to bet that, since the character was distinctive and Willis, at the time, virtually unknown, it was the character David Addison who made the first impression. When Willis moved on to the *Die Hard* films and other roles, it was considered something of a risk, since no one had ever seen him as anything but the comedic Addison character before.

In other words, the first time you "met" Bruce Willis, he was as ingratiating, funny, and "regular guy" as you've *ever* seen him. He made an impression because he was *charming*, and even if it was a fictional character he played, the illusion was good enough to convince millions of Americans. He made a first impression, and it was enough to propel Willis to a career that continues to this day. That's charm.

First Impressions in Business

In business, luckily, meetings are more often planned in advance (although a chance meeting with someone who could become a client, customer, or even an employer are certainly possible). It is, therefore, feasible to train for a first impression, and to make one based on exactly the kind of image you want to project to that person at that time.

I would advise against doing anything like that.

If rehearsing means that you'll have to create a new, false persona for yourself, give the new business associate whatever he or she is looking for, and have to continue to put on that mask every time you come into contact with that person, it is too hard a task for anyone to tackle. You can't possibly maintain a total charade for the years you hope a business relationship will last.

On the other hand, if you are simply using elements of your own personality that you don't normally tap into, if you are making an effort to know what the new associate might want and emphasize that part of yourself, then planning for a first impression makes perfect sense. Again, the key is to know what the other person wants, and deliver it, as is the goal in any business transaction.

Charm in this case means more than learning the newcomer's name. It can't hurt to find out whether your new associate is married, if he has children, or what area of the country (or the world) he might have come from. A little background ahead of time can provide a topic of conversation as well as a strong impression that you've made an effort on the other person's behalf. You want him to like you because you care about him.

Before the meeting begins, it's always a good idea to offer the guest something on arrival—a soft drink or water, coffee or tea are frequent choices—to create an aura of concern and interest. I'm often amazed at how few business meetings begin with some such offer. Even if it is declined, it has made the impression you wanted to make.

Have the agenda ready for the meeting, but unless it's a formal presentation, be prepared for the conversation to veer off the planned course. Answer questions, and *listen* to the questions and comments being made by your guest. If you are the guest at the meeting, be sure to listen to the presentation, and to express your concerns, but also to ask questions that indicate your interest in the subject at hand and the host's point of view.

After the meeting, be sure to thank the new associate for her time and attention. A thank-you card is *essential*. No, an e-mail *won't* do, and yes, it has to be handwritten. A phone call is acceptable, but it doesn't take the place of the thank-you note; it merely enhances the impact of one.

If the meeting is especially important to your business, a thank-you gift is not a bad idea. It doesn't have to be elaborate or expensive, but it should convey the message you're trying to impart—*I care about you and your business*.

Charm isn't merely the witty banter and ingratiating smile we immediately expect when the word is used. It is the intelligent use of attributes you already have to demonstrate your concerns and interests. And in empathizing with your business associate, you make it that much simpler to *be* charming—to show that your interests and concerns in this transaction or partnership take into account the other person's needs as well.

There is no better time than at the first meeting to make that point. Make it without a veneer of artificiality, and you will be considered quite charming. Is that enough to get you to the top of your business? No, but it is an essential place to start.

Chapter 4

Charming Your Way
to the Top

Who are the most successful people in the world, the ones who are at the very pinnacle of their chosen fields? The leaders of countries, of corporations, of artistic and entertainment endeavors? They are, almost exclusively, the most charming and ingratiating people who begin the climb to the top.

Now, it's not possible to rely on charm and charm alone to rise to the peaks of professional accomplishment. On the contrary, if you have no aptitude for what you've decided to try, no amount of charm is going to take you to the highest levels of the business.

Also, I'm not arguing that every head of every company is a charming person. Some of them are famously vindictive, ruthless, and thoroughly despicable, yet they've risen to the top without the minimum daily requirement of charm. How is this possible?

Well, no matter how effective the quality of charm can be—and I believe it is *extremely* effective—it doesn't exist in a vacuum. Human beings are what they are, and some of them have the talent, the intelligence, and the ambition to rise to the top (luck also plays a part in some cases) without using, or in some cases even possessing, a degree of charm. They are the exceptions that underscore the rule.

The point is that charm as a quality of your demeanor, a habit you learn to exercise, is something that can be so beneficial to your success there is no point in *not* knowing how to use it. Even if you are one of those people who have gotten to the top without it, charm can still help you stay where you are.

I had some dealings a number of years ago with a very prominent Hollywood figure, an executive who had reached the very pinnacle of his profession. We met, as I often do with prospective clients, to discuss ways my business could help publicize and improve his image, which was, I'm compelled to say, to the best personally. This was a man more feared than respected.

He asked me to write up a proposal consisting of many of the ideas we had discussed, in the form of a letter to him. This is not typical—it almost constitutes my working for free—but I agreed to write something up and send it to him because I was interested in getting the account.

So I wrote the memo, sent it to the executive's office, and waited. And waited. And waited some more.

I never heard *anything* back from him or his assistants. Finally, after quite a number of days had gone by, I decided to check and make sure the memo had arrived and been seen by the prospective client. His assistant informed me that it was there, and he had seen it. No further information was forthcoming.

Ever.

I never heard another word from the man, and despite my going the extra mile (and a half) to accommodate him, there wasn't so much as a "thank you" involved.

This, I have to say, was not a charming man. And when he soon fell from the lofty heights he had attained, it should be noted, the rest of the Hollywood community made sure to get out of the way so that his landing would be that much harder. Let's say there was no great sobbing heard in Los Angeles when this man was no longer the power he had been. As of this writing, he still is not, and a number of business ventures of his have failed in the interim.

Now, think how things might have been different if this man had made the smallest effort to be charming. First of all, he probably would not have requested that I do some work for him pro bono, especially since he was one of the wealthier men in town at the time. It makes no sense when in a position of power to expect people to grant you favors you don't need.

Second, assuming I had still done the work and sent the memo to his office, a thank-you note (or at the very least, a phone call from an assistant) would have confirmed that my work had not gone unnoticed, or worse, from my perspective, that it had somehow never reached its destination (although I knew through the delivery service I used that it had, and had been signed for in his office). This is a simple, basic, *easy* thing to do, it greatly enhances a businessperson's reputation, and it costs virtually nothing. You'd be amazed how often a thank-you acknowledgment is lacking in virtually every industry operating in this country today.

Is this an example of charm or courtesy? Well, it would *seem* that a thank-you note, call, or (in some cases) e-mail would be a basic, standard procedure, but the sad fact is, it is an exception. It is now seen as going above and beyond the call of duty. It is, if you want to look at it this way, a luxury.

On the other hand, however, most ultrasuccessful people I've met, unlike that Hollywood exec, have been extremely charming, and they know perfectly well that it's one of the qualities that has gotten them to the level of success they've reached. When *Dynasty* was the hottest show on television, I worked extensively with Linda Evans, and she was—and is—one of the most gracious and, yes, charming people I have ever met. At the time, she was the star of one of the biggest hits on television, was world famous, and commanded an impressive salary for her work. In other words, she didn't *have* to be charming; she just was. It came naturally to her.

The question, for people trying to incorporate charm into their business personalities, is *how*. Assuming that charm is not something simply inborn—as it seems to be in a lucky few—but something that can be taught, and more to the point, *learned*, then there has to be a method for acquiring the trait and using it in business situations to help you further your cause.

So, how *do* you charm your way to the top?

First, you have to make that leap and determine that you *can* be charming. Confidence is important, if not essential. And knowing that you can, with practice, learn to use the tools you can acquire is central to the idea of using charm to help improve your business or your career.

That will come with practice, however. Confidence is something that develops naturally when you've performed successfully enough times for the act itself to be second nature. In time, and with enough work, you won't be *acting* like someone who is charming; you *will* be charming.

Initially, observation will be your best friend. Quietly notice the people around you whom you consider to be the most facile, the most confident—but not arrogant—the most agreeable company you know. Don't tell them you're watching them, because then their behavior will become studied and practiced. Just observe your friends or colleagues as they go about the average day. Watch what they do and how they do it. Make note (literally, if need be) of the things they do that you consider especially ingratiating or effective. As Yogi Berra once said, "You can observe a lot just by watching."

What should you be watching for? Unexpected gestures, to begin with. Note what your friend does that is not what you see in the standard human interaction. For example, while seated at a table in a restaurant, most people simply make an order from the server, accept it when it arrives, and pay the bill after it is offered. That's the standard form of interaction.

The charming form might include such additions as asking the server's name, engaging him in conversation, thanking him when the order arrives, and making sure to ask for the bill without the wordless gestures ("writing on a pad") that often accompany such requests across a room.

In fact, restaurants are excellent places to hone one's charm skills. They have a set pattern of situations and conditioned responses, yet they offer plenty of room to vary from the most frequently used avenues. They include a social atmosphere, yet are establishments where business is often transacted. And, since many business meetings are held over food or drinks, they provide an excellent context for later reference when you are putting your skills into practice. But, as a patron in a restaurant you are not a businessperson (assuming the meal is not attached to a business purpose), you can feel free to practice (and in some cases, fail the first time) without any fear of hurting your chances for business success.

Go to the restaurant—and for our purposes, let's make it anything but a fast-food outlet—with a friend or more. In fact, invite people you consider to be the most charming among those you know, but make sure everyone gets along, or you won't have much fun, and the charm will not exactly flow freely.

First, notice how your friends interact with the restaurant's staff. When dealing with the host or hostess, do they simply walk up and say, "four for dinner," or do they engage the greeter in conversation, and how do they start such a conversation? See if they ask the host's or hostess's name, or do they stare at the name tag that might be pinned to the employee's shirt? Do they mention something that everyone in the area might be talking about (the weather, if it is notable, might be one example) while being escorted to a table? The bottom line: Have they made an *impression* by the time the party is seated?

I'm willing to bet the answer to most of those questions—especially the last one—will be "yes." People who use charm effectively are thinking about the other person's needs immediately and constantly. If it's especially hot outside, perhaps the greeter has been hearing that all day. If the host or hostess is asked for recommendations from the menu, that might start a conversation.

But it should be clearly noted that you must never expect someone in a working environment to stop performing his job in order to have a long conversation with you. The key is to be to the point and to make an impression *quickly*, so as to best leave a positive feeling with the employee, associate, or client.

Obviously, when you're in a business meeting or some other planned function, you will have more time to make your impression, and to engage in conversation. But the restaurant is excellent for practice, and the practice can be continued with the server.

Often in today's restaurants, the server introduces herself at tableside, but if no introduction is made, it always helps to ask. Not only does this make the server feel like you care—the cardinal rule of charming your way to the top—but it also makes it easier, as you repeat the name, to remember it as time goes on.

Again, finding out something about your server is helpful. If a sporting event or election is making news, you might make reference to it—but *not* if you're going to express a preference for one side or the other. It's a way to start a conversation, but the last thing you want is an argument.

If the server is in the midst of an extremely busy crunch time, you don't want to start a long involved conversation. Just make sure you make an impression, listen to what the other person says, and then *make a reference to it later* so she knows you were paying attention.

For example, if you begin by talking to the server about particular choices on the menu, and she makes a recommendation, if you order that dish, you might want to thank her for that suggestion after you are finished eating. It provides a reference to something you have already discussed, and acknowledges something another person did for you, making her feel appreciated. It also enhances the server's feeling about her job—she's done it well.

Naturally, if the suggestion made was a poor one, you might not want to be effusive in your praise, but the key is not to make the server feel like she has failed—her taste and yours simply didn't mesh.

Don't practice charm simply on the staff, however. Observe your friends or colleagues as they interact with each other. If someone does something especially ingratiating, or especially irritating, take note of it. You don't have to react immediately, but you might want to discuss it quietly with that person later.

Also, observe the effect your behavior, whether it is obvious or not, is having on the group. Do they seem to be enjoying your company, or are they ignoring what you say (although charming people would never do that)? Do you feel at any time like something you've said or done was inappropriate? Again, you might want to take note of that and seek out one of your closer friends in the group later to discuss it.

Charm in business begins with charm in overall behavior. So people who begin to observe what is and is not charming in every aspect of daily life have a better chance to apply those skills to the business environment.

You *can* charm your way to the top. You have to do it in steps, and some of them will be small, but they are all significant.

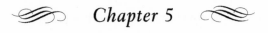

Chapter 5

Nuts and Bolts
and Baby Steps

Charm is an art and a craft—it is something that can be practiced and learned, but also something that comes to some people naturally. Those who are "born" with charm continue to have to practice; they will not be able to maintain a charming reputation without constant tune-ups.

For those of us (and I count myself among what I consider to be the majority) not blessed with an inordinate amount of natural charm, the task may seem daunting at the outset. How, after all, can you practice to act like something is happening naturally?

Well, actors do it all the time. Those "natural" moments you see on-screen or onstage have been written, memorized, rehearsed, and discussed to the point of minutiae; they are moments that are *made* to seem spontaneous and "real." You can do the same with your quest to learn how to be charming.

The easiest (and best) thing is to learn by example. As we've discussed in previous chapters, the first step is to identify those people you know whom you consider to be especially charming, and observe how they handle various situations. You don't have to emulate the actions exactly—particularly since each situation is unique, and you are unlikely to run into exactly the same set of circumstances—but you can see how people you watch manage to convince whomever they're dealing with that they care about the other's problem, and how it comes across as charming and endearing.

For example, the doorman in my building is an elegant fellow named Odis, and I have observed him for a good number of years. Odis is absolutely masterly at conveying concern for everyone who enters or leaves the building. He's especially good at gauging your mood, and knowing when to step forward and when to leave you alone.

"Some people don't want to talk to you when they get home," he says. "You see from their face what kind of day they had, and if they don't want to talk, you back off."

Especially important to the decision-making process here is *observation*. It seems a simple thing to gauge a person's mood from the look on his face, but in our coarse, vulgar society, we have learned to do anything *but* look someone in the face. We have learned that making eye contact with strangers leads to uncomfortable encounters, if not outright danger. In other words, we are trained from childhood to avoid others, and certainly not to try to exercise charm with those we don't know.

Odis, partially because of the work he does, but mostly because of the kind of man he is, makes sure to look into the face of everyone entering or leaving the building. Yes, part of that is a security measure— he is the first line of defense for the building—but part of it is his desire to help, particularly those who might not be having the best time of things right now.

Charm, after all, is the art of caring. A key attribute to cultivate is *empathy*, the ability to put yourself into the other guy's shoes and feel what it would be like to have to deal with his life for a while. Consider that, and even if your burden is worse than the other person's, at least you will understand the motivations of his actions. It will help you be a better person, and it will be an enormous advantage in business dealings.

Some businesspeople I know consider empathy to be a weakness, and I can't understand that point of view at all. For those who believe that in order to be a success in business, "you have to be a killer," I offer an alternate theory. I believe that in order to be a success in business, you have to be a *lifesaver*, someone who understands and solves the problems of the client, the associate, or the employee. Otherwise, why would anyone employ you?

To do that, you must cultivate and exercise empathy.

Consider: Is that cashier at the supermarket slow because she's lazy, or because it's her first day on the job? Is your colleague at work really trying to undermine your authority, or does he simply not understand his own responsibilities? Does your employee show up late every day because he's irresponsible, or because he's trying to raise two children on his own and has trouble getting out the door on time?

If you can see the other person's side of the equation, you are well on your way to utilizing empathy effectively. Now, some people really *are* lazy, irresponsible, and undermining, but if you can discern each person's motivations, you will be much more likely to find out which colleagues are sincerely trying to do the job, and which ones are not cut out for this business.

My friend Odis, one of the most charming people I know, is a whiz at reading other people, and he knows who needs help and who prefers to be left alone. I observe him to pick up some of the same skills for my own use, and even if I don't take to it naturally, I can certainly learn the techniques and apply them with a good deal of practice.

The best writers, directors, and actors are also experts at pinpointing the forces that drive other people. Think about how many times you've heard an actor, during an interview, talk about finding the "character's motivation." That's another way of saying the actor is trying to see the character's side of the story, whether the hero or the villain (or someone in between), to best understand how to embody that character. Bela Lugosi didn't *really* sleep in a coffin and attack women at night. Robert DeNiro doesn't drive around Manhattan with a Mohawk haircut looking for people to shoot. Even Harrison Ford doesn't fly from place to place cracking a bullwhip and looking for lost antiquities.

These actors needed to understand what the person who was created on the script page before them *wanted*, and *why* they would do the things they were required to do in the story. For some actors, this process includes writing a lengthy "backstory," explaining the character's life long before the story begins, to better explain what drives the character into the action described. This helps the actor understand the character, and so the character's actions, even if they are not the kinds of things the actor himself would do, are justified to the actor.

You can do the same kind of thing when you're trying to understand the people you encounter in your everyday life. Combine curiosity with observation, and you will begin to understand other people's motivations. Once you can determine that the newsstand man is always gruff in the morning because he hates getting up before dawn, or that the vice president above you on the corporate ladder is dealing with a health issue, and *that's* why she's been distant lately, you can begin to use your observations to better establish yourself as a charming, ingratiating, *helpful* person.

Remember the concept of *baby steps*. You can't solve the problems of everyone you've ever met on your first day. Odds are, you can't solve everyone's problems no matter how many years you can devote to the pursuit. But you *can* offer a kind word, a bit of assistance, even a smile to help make the impression you're striving to create.

In fact, a smile is one of the most basic and important building blocks of charm. That is, a *sincere* smile is extremely useful and charming. A *phony* one is the absolute polar opposite of charming—it is off-putting, obnoxious, and repellent. So, how do you know when to smile?

It doesn't have to be a time when you're especially happy—it can just be one when you're not *unhappy*. That's a place to begin. *Always* smile when meeting a new person, because you never know who your best friend is going to be. People want to feel like you're glad to see them, so smile when they enter a room. Obviously, this doesn't mean you should grin like a jack o' lantern every time a complete stranger passes by, but when you do happen to catch someone's eye, a smile is a considerable improvement over no smile at all.

People really do respond to such small adjustments. Try smiling at a few people you pass on the street tomorrow morning. Not a wide grin that looks pasted on, just a pleasant, "glad-to-see-you" type of smile that can be read and absorbed quickly. You don't have to stop and strike up a conversation with any one of the people at whom you're smiling; just acknowledge their presence and move on.

Next, consider the first impression you're going to make when meeting someone new. What would you want said to you at that occasion? "Nice to meet you?" "Finally!" or "So this is the person I've been hearing so much about?"

Any of these is acceptable, depending on the circumstances involved. If, indeed, you have been dealing with a business associate online or on the phone for a long time, and this is your first face-to-face meeting, "Finally!" could be an appropriate opening line. If you are truly dealing with this person for the first time in any medium, then something more innocuous like "Pleased to meet you" would be safer.

But the key is *not* to think about what you would like to hear back at you. The center of charm is to consider what the *other* person would want. What do you know about this person? In some cases, the only thing you know is what function the person serves professionally—if you're walking into the dry cleaner's and meet the person behind the counter, you know nothing except that this is a person who works at the dry cleaning store you patronize.

In those cases, you have two avenues of conversation: you can ask about the job the person is performing, or you can confine yourself to general topics anyone can relate to.

Light conversation is a skill and an art—it requires a little thought, and quick reactions. But it is not difficult and it is not dangerous. Asking people how their day is going is a simple and quick way to start a conversation, and—especially—to demonstrate that you are interested in *them*, in their feelings and problems, at least on a very limited basis. I'm not talking about the robotic "have-a-nice-day" kind of communication that is clearly rehearsed and insincere. In this case, the easiest thing at the dry cleaner, the supermarket, the restaurant, or the bookstore is simply to look the person behind the counter in the eye, smile, and ask, "How's your day going?"

It's that simple. And because we live in the kind of society I've described, you have already distinguished yourself from the vast majority of people who walk into this establishment every day. You're already considered charming, simply because you took the time to ask about another person's welfare.

This same kind of scenario can be used in your business dealings. When meeting a potential client, employer, or colleague for the first time, begin with the sincere inquiry into that person's day.

But here's the key—*listen to the answer*. Too often, we go through life on autopilot, listening to the same cues and giving the same responses: "How are you?" "Fine, and you?" "Good." To be considered charming, and to use your charm to better your position in business, you have to get beyond programmed answers and actually listen to what's being said. Be observant. If someone looks tired, you can either be insulting ("Geez, you look awful!") or concerned ("Is there anything I can help with?"). Guess which one is going to be better received?

Small talk is actually misnamed. There is nothing small about asking after a colleague's welfare, nothing at all trivial about expressing concern and interest in someone else's life. It is the *attitude* that most people bring to this practice, the feeling of ritual rather than experience, that trivializes the practice.

The celebrities I have represented, from Vanna White to Fleetwood Mac, have always understood the power of small talk. Someone who is world famous values it more, because so much of what they do is watched and scrutinized. Fans meeting famous entertainers value their few minutes, or seconds, and rehearse their lines long before the meeting, in some cases. The level of actual conversation is minimal. So when someone actually asks after a celebrity's welfare sincerely, it is a special moment that distinguishes itself from the rest.

Now, don't get me wrong. I'm not arguing that entertainers have awful lives. In fact, they are treated about as well as anyone on this planet. But their lives tend to be insulated from the rest of the world, and when they make real contact with someone new, that can make a huge difference to them.

Stars have often gotten where they are in part because of their charm. I'm not arguing that people at the top of the entertainment ladder aren't there because of their talent—if they couldn't act, sing, dance, or tell jokes, no amount of charm could have propelled them to the top. But because they exercised charm, in many cases, the road to the top was a little smoother than it might have been otherwise.

Of course, some entertainers do not practice charm, and feel they are entitled to better treatment than everyone else. When Michael Jackson requires the crew of his music video to avoid looking directly at him, that is not charming. Some people, on every level of society, live outside the norms. There are exceptions, in other words, to every rule.

The key to any exchange between people, however, is *sincerity*. If people believe you are merely mouthing the words you think they want to hear so you can benefit, your charm will fall flat on the ground, and you will be considered as, believe me, less than charming. There's nothing worse than someone considered to be duplicitous or "phony." So sincerity is extremely important, and the next topic we will discuss.

Chapter 6

Sincerity, and How to Fake It

There's an old saw, attributed to everyone from Groucho Marx to Richard Nixon, that goes something like this: "Sincerity is key. Once you can fake that, you've got it made."

Because so many people mistake the proper definition of charm—they think it means being glib, smooth, and shallow—another common misconception is that charm means being insincere. Nothing could be farther from the truth.

The fact is, charm is all *about* sincerity. It is the fact that a person can convey an honest interest in another's life that makes him charming, and without the honesty, there is no charm. There may be the *appearance* of charm if the person faking it is skillful enough, but *real* charm is another matter, and can't be simulated.

This leads to a classic business problem. How to summon honest, sincere concern for another's problems when you either don't know

that person or, under more difficult circumstances, know him, and dislike him intensely.

While this sounds like it is a cynical, even frivolous, problem, it is
real. We're not going to be close friends with *every* business associate,
every client, *every* employee. It's just not possible in the course of
actual human relations. But in business, it is necessary to treat each
person we meet as a friend, no matter how much that goes against
the reality of the actual situation. If we adopt the 10 Commandments
of Charming Your Way to the Top, it becomes an even more central
issue.

The 10 Commandments of
Charming Your Way to the Top

1. Thou shalt always convey interest in the other person's
concerns.
2. Thou shalt always show sympathy for the other person's
problems.
3. Thou shalt always send thank-you notes. Yes, always.
4. Thou shalt follow up with phone calls.
5. Thou shalt pick up the check, when thou invites.
6. Thou shalt smile most of the time.
7. Thou shalt make eye contact.
8. Thou shalt remember—and use—the other person's
name.
9. Thou shalt be on time, when thou can't be early.
10. Thou shalt mean what thou sayeth.

That last commandment is the one we're examining most closely
here. If you don't mean what you say—if you can be detected, even without evidence, in a lie, your charm is not only suspect, it is eradicated.

So, how do you go about expressing sincere concern to those back-stabbing, lying, cheating swine who compete against you, or are after your job?

It's human nature to be less than thrilled with those who are—or seem to be—in opposition to us. Competition and business realities conspire to make us behave with less than total courtesy—forget *charm*—to those we see as working against us in one way or another. But as Katharine Hepburn noted in *The African Queen*, "Nature is what we are put on this Earth to rise above."

Not to mention, it's just plain bad business to treat *anyone* rudely, no matter what offense we might have perceived or threat we envision. If business is a competition (and it is), we can win by being more charming and getting more business than our competitors. Living well, I believe someone else once said, is the best revenge.

It's helpful, then, to remember that charm and courtesy, used together even when the recipient is a competitor or rival, can lead to rewards for the user. Think of each smile as a small step toward a higher goal in your career, each compliment paid as an investment in your business.

Naturally, it's easier to use charm when your recipient is someone for whom you feel genuine regard and respect, but that's not always going to be the case. When you are doing something helpful for a colleague or ally, it probably won't be as essential to focus on your own goals, since you'll know instinctively that helping this person will not only feel good because it's the right thing to do, it will plant a seed that your ally will undoubtedly use to help you at a later date.

In other words, when your friend is being charmed, you don't need to fake it.

Now, don't misunderstand—under no circumstances would I ever advise you to lie in business dealings of any sort. That is not only bad business, it's just plain wrong, and in many cases, can be criminal. Lying is *not* part of Charming Your Way to the Top, and never will be.

Remember that the difference between courtesy and charm can be illustrated by the example of holding an elevator door open for someone rushing for the door. Keeping the door open is *courtesy*. If, once the person is inside, you compliment his or her clothing, that's *charm*.

BUT. It's only charm if you *mean* it. Say your colleague getting on the elevator is dressed in something that makes her look ludicrous, and you compliment the outfit, not only will you look like a duplicitous fool, you'll also point out to her something that will make her feel that much *less* confident and positive. Lying is the opposite of charm.

When you're dealing with someone you see as a competitor or a rival, or someone you simply don't like, don't offer an obviously false compliment. Don't smile an artificial, cynical smile. You can't allow yourself the luxury of a really satisfying sneer or a cutting remark. Charm, after all, is not about you—it's about the people with whom you are dealing.

So, no matter what the circumstances or the cast of characters, your priority (when deciding to exhibit your charm for the benefit of your career) is to make sure the other person knows you are concerned with his problems, worries, questions, and desires. You are not necessarily going to solve all those problems, calm all those worries, answer all those questions, or fulfill all those desires, but you are certainly going to listen to them with a genuine interest and do your best to be as much help as you can. That's the base definition of charm.

Given that, and given that you're dealing with someone you'd rather not, the key in maintaining the charming attitude is to empathize as thoroughly as you can and consider what this person—even this person who might be working against your best interests—needs from the business dealings you're doing. Assuming that his goal is not in conflict with yours—that is, you certainly are not required to do something that will do your business or your career harm—you can still fulfill the requirements of charm. Start with courtesy, and then consider what more there is to do.

There's nothing hard, for example, about sending a thank-you note to someone you don't particularly like. There's nothing damaging about paying for a lunch, even if the other person is wealthier than you. It won't hurt to smile, shake hands, and discuss a business situation with someone whose motives may not be the same as your own.

But if there is one skill that is most closely associated with charm, it is the ability to *listen*, and that is without question the simplest, least expensive, and most effective component of a relationship in a business or personal context. It costs exactly nothing, and can give you so many advantages, it seems almost too obvious to count them.

1. Listening tells the other person you care about his concerns—the very basis of charm.
2. Listening enables you to understand more about the person to whom you're talking—friend or foe. You can gain valuable information that can be useful in later dealings.
3. Listening demonstrates charm, as it de-emphasizes your interest in yourself, and focuses on someone else.
4. Listening reveals no secrets of yours, betrays no trust, costs nothing, and divulges no strategy.
5. Listening helps develop your reputation as someone who can put ego aside and really commit his resources to another. That's charm.

What listening does for a businessperson is to provide information and convey interest. At its core, that is about as powerful a one-two punch as can be found in the business world.

Remember, charm is a much more *proactive* thing than courtesy. Charm does not wait for a situation to arise; it creates the situation. Charm does not react; it acts.

So, when dealing with others in *any* context, charm will be sincere. Not "sincere," as so many people use it, meaning that one is *pretending* to care, but truly sincere. You really *should* care about what is being said to you, no matter who is doing the talking.

Remember, it can have a huge impact on your future. The next great idea, the next enormous opportunity, is not going to be presented with a fanfare from a marching band and a banner proclaiming "NEXT GREAT IDEA!!!!" It will probably be dropped into a conversation as an off-hand remark, an afterthought, a casual comment. There might even be a veiled threat in some remarks that can be fought off if attention is paid early enough.

Listening, in other words, is absolutely invaluable.

Even if there *isn't* a tremendous nugget of information in the conversation, there is much that can be gained by someone who is paying enough attention to be considered charming. Like the other person's *name*.

Sure, it seems like a small thing, but people like to hear their names. They like it when a new acquaintance takes the time and makes the effort to learn and remember their names. They like to hear their names repeated back, as a reminder that the new acquaintance (friend?) cares enough to pay attention.

I once conducted an interview with Sherry Lansing, the president of Paramount Pictures, and arguably the most powerful woman in Hollywood. And I noticed throughout the evening, which was well attended, that Ms. Lansing never failed to respond with the name of the person to whom she was talking.

"Thank you, Michael," she said as she was leaving. "I must tell you, Michael, that it was a wonderful evening. Michael, I'm sorry I have to run, but I really appreciate all you've done. Take care, Michael."

That doesn't translate as well in print as it does in conversation, but it is a very charming trait. Using (and remembering) someone's name—particularly someone you don't know well—is a sign that you care enough to pay attention to that person, and that the person matters enough to you that you will take the time and make the effort.

It is very charming, and clearly quite memorable. It's a skill to cultivate and practice, so that it sounds as sincere as you hope it will be when you use it.

Also, using that technique when leaving voice mail or telephone answering machine messages is a very telling, important point. Yes, identify yourself, but make sure you speak *directly to the person for whom you're leaving the message, and use his name*. It shows that even during unguarded moments you are thinking of someone other than yourself.

Sincerity is, in the final analysis, something that *can't* be faked, and that is all for the best. It can be nurtured and cultivated, however, so that it is more expertly and honestly expressed, to maximize the effect it can have on business associates, friends, and acquaintances. Charm is, when boiled down to its essence, caring, and sincerity is the clearest sign of caring.

It doesn't mean that every honest thought coming through your head should be expressed uncensored—that's not sincerity; it's merely bluntness and can be the least charming thing on the planet—but that the concern that you show, the interest you express toward another person, be real and genuine.

I make a point of noting the birthday of almost everyone with whom I do business. On those days, which I have written down or noted on my computer, I make a point of calling them to say happy birthday. I mean it sincerely; I hope they do have happy birthdays.

That doesn't take much time out of my day and it costs me very little. But it means so much to many of the people I call that I can hear the honest surprise in their voices. "How did you *remember?*" they'll ask. (It's not that hard—I just wrote the date down on a calendar.) And I have made an impression that will color everything that comes after it.

It was an honest, sincere gesture and it had a positive effect on my relationship with another person, one with whom I hope to do business again. Is that so difficult?

Chapter 7

Living a Charmed Life

Business isn't just something that happens from nine to five anymore, if in fact it ever was. We are in our professions and our jobs every minute of every day, with time out to sleep (usually) and occasionally, to take a shower. But the fact is, we're probably thinking about business then, too.

If charm is to be a part of our business plan (and it should be), then we are bound to continue to work at being charming twenty-four hours a day, seven days a week. There is no time out, even when we are not necessarily concentrating our efforts on business. A potential client might be met at our child's soccer game, and a good business idea could very well come to us over breakfast, even if we're not having a "power breakfast" with clients or colleagues.

So how hard is it going to be, then, to keep up the charm 24/7? Won't the occasional crack show through? Won't we sometimes be something less than the most charming people we can possibly be?

Of course we will. Nobody is going to be charming every second of every day; everyone is going to have the occasional bad mood, angry moment, or exhausting day. You can't beat yourself up over not being perfect—so far, virtually no one has managed that particular feat, depending on which religion happens to be your own.

Still, maintaining the charming lifestyle throughout the course of quite a normal day can be trying, even for those to whom it comes naturally. Life is full of disappointments, difficulties, and disasters. And even when those aren't present, we deal every day with minor annoyances, irritations, and the tiny pains that come with being a member of an impolite, discourteous, un-charming society. After a long day of those, even Mr. Rogers probably came home cranky once in a while.

But consider this: even after a long day, even after the usual trials and tribulations of our society have had their shots, some people really *do* manage to remain charming. And, as with all truly charming people, they seem to do it effortlessly, naturally and sincerely, even when they might be seeing red over the slow line at the supermarket or the rude cab driver they just met on the way home.

I live in a high-rise apartment building in Los Angeles, and at the end of a relatively long day recently, got on the elevator to make that last leg of my journey home. A woman of Middle Eastern descent and her mother were in the elevator.

When I first entered the elevator, they were engaged in a conversation in their native language. I thought nothing of this—I was not expecting to be included in the talk, and just wanted to get home. But after a few moments, the younger woman turned to me and apologized for keeping me excluded by speaking in a language I clearly did not understand.

"I really didn't expect you to do anything else," I told her.

"Still," she replied, "it's rude to do that to someone, and I'm sorry. It's just that my mother does not speak English very well."

I thought that was the ultimate in charm—even though there was a perfectly good reason for these two women to be conversing in a language I can't speak, she felt it was important to apologize to me for the way I must have felt. This was an example of someone thinking about how the other person must feel, and making an adjustment to accommodate those feelings. That is charm, and it came at the end of the day, when nerves are a little bit more raw.

There's no reason we can't keep up the charm, particularly after we've had a reasonable time to practice. Business requires us to at least attempt charming behavior for much of our day, but those of us who *don't* give in to the impulse to relax and let down our guard when we're "off duty" are the ones who are truly, sincerely charming.

It's not as difficult as it sounds—as with any other skill, charm becomes second nature with enough practice. And the more you practice, the more natural the execution becomes.

A Profile in Charm: The Painting Waiter

There is a restaurant not far from where I live, where an artist is paying his bills by working as a waiter. It's not an uncommon situation. How many waiters in New York or Los Angeles (or any number of other cities) are aspiring actors, writers, directors, singers, or sculptors? It seems, sometimes, that finding a waiter who is a *waiter* is a rarity to be cherished and nurtured.

In most of these cases, the aspiring artist (of whichever art happens to apply) is unhappy about having to work serving food when she could be painting, acting, or practicing what the individual sees as her true calling. Often, these people are surly, inattentive, and sometimes downright rude, feeling they are somehow being forced to sully their talent by serving the public. You've run into hundreds of such waiters (or counter help, or clerks) in your lifetime, so you can probably spot one across a crowded restaurant.

This particular artist, however, is none of those things. He makes it a point to charm each and every diner who sits at his table, and is an excellent server. But there's something else, as well.

With each bill he delivers, the waiter also offers a tiny watercolor, hand-painted during his breaks—gratis. Each customer is made to feel special in this way, catered to by someone who is indeed an artist, but doesn't gripe about the circumstances that force him to work in another profession.

Is there a benefit to the waiter/artist, too? Does he manage to have his art seen by hundreds of patrons, some of whom might be impressed enough to investigate further? Do his tips increase with the obvious attention he has paid his tables?

Of course. There's an upside for the waiter. And his tips are perhaps double those of the rest of the wait staff in that restaurant on any given night. He has made an impression—and a positive one that will be well remembered after the dinner is long forgotten.

But the key? He says that even if his tips were not increased, he'd do the little watercolors anyway.

That is charm in the marketplace. That is the idea of distinguishing oneself through an act that is selfless and unique, something that empathizes with restaurant patrons who might get a little extra enjoyment out of their dinner with a hand-painted souvenir. It is the kind of gesture that would be *so easy* not to make. No one would notice if there was no watercolor with the check, since no one would routinely expect such a thing. There is no reason for this waiter to make this gesture, except that he wants to do the best he can in his own way.

And he teaches us a great lesson in charm.

Thinking about someone else's concerns is a freeing, liberating experience. It allows you to let go of your own worries for a moment, pretend they don't exist, and take on the thoughts of another human being. It can clear your mind and help you to think more freely and accurately about yourself when you begin to do that again.

Also, taking on another's concerns is a great advantage in virtually any interpersonal relationship. Empathy for a friend's feelings will help to strengthen the relationship and convey the message that you are someone who can be trusted, and whose friendship is valuable. This could mean a good deal to you when it is *your* turn to have a problem that might require a friend's assistance.

In a romantic relationship, empathy is perhaps the most valuable tool you can possibly develop. Anticipating another's needs or wants can greatly increase the chances that the other person will think highly of you, which is extremely important, especially at the beginning of the relationship. If you can determine what the other person needs emotionally, and provide that, you have a good chance of developing a very strong romantic relationship.

But in a business relationship, empathy is a tool and a weapon. Make no mistake: competition is real and ferocious in *every* business, and being able to spot and use an advantage can be the key to survival, or success. Place yourself in your competitor's mindset before he has time to act, and you may be able to fend off an attack or a strategy that could be used against you.

Now, since charm is based on empathy, and since we are discussing the possibility of maintaining charm at all times, it seems that there would be no time for you to think your *own* thoughts and deal with your *own* problems. That's not the case at all; of course you are always living in your own mind.

The key is to know when to exercise your capacity to empathize. This, again, is something you'll develop with practice, but it is a central skill to acquire.

In business, some things will remain constant. For example, if you own a chain of ice cream stores, your customers' needs will usually be pretty uniform—they want ice cream, they want a choice of flavors, and they want fast, courteous service, and a clean environment. You don't have to think about those things all the time, since you can assume that each customer who walks in the door will want them.

So, once your business is established, those concerns will require maintenance, but they won't have to be the top priorities all the time. Only when there are signs that one of your core concerns is beginning to deteriorate, such as reports from customers that the stores are not as clean as they once were, will you have to attend to these concerns (of course, attending to them *before* customers begin to notice would be much better, but still, if a strong system is in place, these things should run themselves fairly smoothly).

This leaves you time to think about other issues related to your business: What is the competition doing, and how are they reacting to your business? What more could your customers want that you're not yet delivering? How can you increase your employees' productivity by accommodating some of their needs and insisting they accommodate those of the business at the same time? These are the kinds of things that can benefit from your capacity to put yourself in another's shoes and concern yourself with his concerns.

How does your professional life merge with your personal life? Friends are allies, and in business, allies are desperately important. Also, the techniques you use to be charming to friends, relatives, and lovers are the same ones you'll need to know in order to charm your way to the top in business.

But, increasingly, the line between the personal and the professional is blurring. Those who own their own businesses can attest to the idea that there no longer exist such things as "business hours" or "business relationships." Every relationship and every problem is related to business these days.

You must be cognizant of that fact as you deal with people throughout the course of any day. What seems like a purely personal encounter might very well become a business conversation in the blink of an eye, and you have to be prepared for that. Only by practicing the art of empathy, the ability to see things from another's perspective, will you be able to anticipate every situation and use it to your advantage.

For example, if you are having a casual conversation with a friend about her upcoming vacation, it might occur to you that she's leaving for the airport at an inconvenient time. If you have a client who owns a limousine service, perhaps you can arrange a discounted ride to the airport. Or if you work with someone at an airline, maybe you can find a more conveniently scheduled flight for her to take.

That is an example of anticipating another's need before she asks for help, and volunteering your own business connection to help a friend. Now, you have cemented your relationship with your friend more solidly than before, and possibly gained a new customer for a client of yours. The personal relationship and the business relationship have merged, and you have strengthened both.

On another front, perhaps you had a romantic relationship with someone a few years ago that ended for one reason or another. If you were not concerned with charm and acted acrimoniously at the time, you are probably no longer in contact with your former lover. But, if you ended the relationship amicably (thinking of the other person's feelings, even as you have to protect your own), you may still be in contact. At the least, your former love will answer the phone if you call.

If that person is now employed in a business that may be able to use your services or products, you have a contact. If you can find a use for the company your former lover now represents, perhaps you can send some business to that company, and maybe get a better deal than someone with no connections at all.

Personal business, in other words, is exactly that—business. And since charm is the key to success in business, as we have demonstrated here, it can also serve in personal relationships, since they may very well intersect with business interests at any moment.

The most important element, of course, will be your ability to consider what other people will need or want, and to act upon that knowledge to your own benefit.

Think about the artist who works as a waiter. He knows that his patrons may not *need* a new watercolor with every meal, but he knows even better that such a gesture will make him stand out, and might very well make the difference between a negative and a positive impression of the service—and the business—he represents.

He has found a way to brighten other people's days using his own unique talents, and to make them think of him in a positive light. That is about as charming an idea as I can possibly imagine.

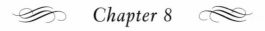

Chapter 8

The Charming Top 50

Words tell, but stories sell.

It's one thing to know on an intellectual basis that charm can help you in business, and to learn the principles of charm and how to apply them. It's another thing, however, and possibly a more powerful one, to have examples of charm to which we can all point.

Everyone learns by example. Our first lessons, to walk, to talk, to behave, are learned from our parents or caregivers. Later on, there are teachers who *tell* us how to behave, but our peers and our family *show* us how to behave.

We learn, also, from public examples: political leaders, actors and actresses whose work we admire, and those in fields we find especially fascinating—astronauts, inventors, craftspeople. We choose our heroes, and we emulate them, even if it is not a conscious decision to do so.

I believe that we learn a good deal about charm by noticing it in others and imitating what they do, the things that especially impress us. So let us consider what I call the "Charming Top 50," a group of people who are especially noteworthy for their charm.

Many names on the list are those of actors and actresses, people who work in the entertainment business. Others are politicians, and still others have done work in other fields. I don't claim to know more than a few of them on a personal level, and I certainly wouldn't presume to say I know anything about the vast majority other than the image they project through their work. But since that is the very thing that we observe and emulate, that is what we will concern ourselves with. For all I know, each and every one goes home and kicks the dog at night, but from the perspective of the public, these are among the most charming people around, and each can teach us a valuable lesson about charming your way to the top.

The Charming Top 50
(In no particular order)

1. **Hugh Grant.** Public scandals aside, in his work, Mr. Grant is among the most charming of all men, even when portraying cads and shallow aging adolescents. Audiences just love him, no matter what part he happens to be playing. His looks don't hurt, but there are a lot of handsome men who wouldn't be as effective. Why? Because Grant is always thinking about the audience, and his anticipation of what we are thinking shades his performance.

2. **Bill Clinton.** Wherever one stands on his politics, his public foibles, or his moral choices—the one thing everyone who ever met our former president face-to-face will agree upon is that when he's talking to you, you are sure to be the foremost thing

on his mind. He conveys this with every look, with a remarkable ability to listen and with obvious attention to your concerns. You may not have supported Clinton, but he is charming.

3. **Paul McCartney.** Think about this—he's among the richest entertainers in the world, was a central member of the most famous act in the history of show business and is the most commercially successful songwriter of *all time*. So how does McCartney keep in touch with the people who buy his records? He always exudes a "regular guy" charm that is clearly well cultivated, raised his children out of the spotlight and makes it a point to talk to the press on common-ground terms. His official title is "Sir Paul," but to a few generations, he's still the "Cute One."

4. **Mary Tyler Moore.** Okay, so she turned the world on with her smile. For encores, she took on dramatic roles that played against type. But in her brutally honest interviews, discussing her son's death or her own alcoholism, she was never anything less than real. She was someone who could have been us, and that image is as charming as can be. For a beautiful woman blessed with enormous talent, identifying with the audience is no small feat of charm.

5. **Walter Cronkite.** They called him "Uncle Walter." They also called him the "Most Trusted Man in America," and there was serious talk at one time about trying to get him to run for president. Much more than a newsreader, Cronkite gave off such honesty and absolute integrity that people turned to him when there was a crisis. If trust is a sign of charm, he had bags of it.

6. **Tom Hanks.** He is such a nice guy that when he gives an interview and says he's *not* such a nice guy, it is accepted as a sign of what a nice guy he is. Even when playing an underworld hit

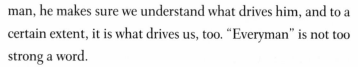

man, he makes sure we understand what drives him, and to a certain extent, it is what drives us, too. "Everyman" is not too strong a word.

7. **Sherry Lansing.** Arguably the most powerful woman in Hollywood is also one of the most charming. In a position (president of Paramount Studios) where she doesn't *have* to be charming (and so many in similar positions make it a point not to be), she always acknowledges the other person, is polite to a fault, and listens attentively to your point. Perhaps the most telling type of charm is the type that is shown when the charmer doesn't *want* anything from you.

8. **Arnold Schwarzenegger.** Armed with a thick accent, no political experience, and a reputation as a man who shoots first and never asks questions, he quite frankly charmed the voters of California into making him their governor. That's a major example of charming your way to the top.

9. **Jon Stewart.** How many people could spend ten minutes on television mercilessly making fun of newsmakers, and then invite them in to sit on his couch and chat about the affairs of the day? Stewart is never anything but polite to his guests, even when it's clear he disagrees with them. And that has helped him book guests ranging from Angelina Jolie to Henry Kissinger.

10. **Bill Cosby.** The first African-American star of a television series in the 1960s morphed himself into America's Favorite Dad in the 1980s by ignoring race and celebrating heritage. He did it by emphasizing the similarities in all our lives and by performing the most charming act imaginable—he made us laugh.

11. **Meg Ryan.** If Mary Pickford was the first actress to bear the title "America's Sweetheart," Ryan was surely the most beloved for

the longest time. Even playing roles that broke out of her romantic-comedy mold, she looked us in the eye and made us love her just by being who she was. That's charm.

12. **Superman.** Let's face it: here's a guy who could have taken over the planet if he felt like it, and there wouldn't have been a thing we could have done to stop him. Instead, he chose to help us whenever he could. Talk about thinking about the other person's concerns!

13. **Jack Lemmon.** Before there was Tom Hanks, there was Jack Lemmon. Able to perform comedy or drama with equal skill, Lemmon could instantly make an audience identify with him because he reacted as we would react. That's empathy, and that's charm.

14. **Wayne Newton.** You don't have to like his act. You don't have to know any of his songs. All you need to know about Wayne Newton is this: he packs the house in Vegas *every night* because he makes his audiences feel special. If every entertainer was this charming, there wouldn't be enough venues for them all to play.

15. **George W. Bush.** In an election where he was perceived as the candidate with less experience and fewer credentials, the one thing that was evident was that he was winning people over through sheer force of personality. The current sitting president is one who knows how to connect with Americans, whether they agree with his policies or not.

16. **Al Hirschfeld.** He had a job that could have turned him into the most mean-spirited man in the world, one that could have made people despise him—drawing caricatures of the celebrated. Emphasizing facial features that could have been embarrassing to performers, Hirschfeld worked with such

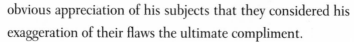

obvious appreciation of his subjects that they considered his exaggeration of their flaws the ultimate compliment.

17. **Julie Andrews.** Come on. *Mary Poppins? The Sound of Music?* This is the woman who told us that a spoonful of sugar would help the medicine go down, and that we should climb every mountain. Even when she bared her breasts in a satire of Hollywood (*S.O.B.*), we felt she was doing it against her will. She was "our Julie."

18. **Joe Torre.** The New York Yankees once went through managers the way most people go through gym socks. Then came the man the tabloids called "Clueless Joe," and with his calm demeanor and his absolute refusal to say anything bad about anybody, he held the job for nine years (and counting) and won four World Series. You can't get much more charming, or to a higher top, than that.

19. **Derek Jeter.** As Torre taught, Jeter learned. Blessed with tremendous athletic ability and good looks, he could have been the most obnoxious baseball player in history. Instead, the multimillionaire who still calls his manager "Mr. Torre" is modest and unassuming. And he was made captain of the most famous team in sports.

20. **Fred Rogers.** He couldn't sing, dance, or tell jokes. He couldn't act. What he could do was talk to children. And he did it in a way that was so endearing, so ingratiating, and so soothing that Mr. Rogers was given a television neighborhood for upward of thirty years. Even after his death, he continues to charm new generations of children in reruns.

21. **Reese Witherspoon.** Playing a role that could have been dismissed as another "dumb blonde," Witherspoon found the humanity and grit in a character who was nothing like her.

She is one of the new breed of actresses who are quickly becoming brands in Hollywood, and her brand is charming, with a capital C.

22. **Dick Van Dyke.** Besides being a gifted physical comedian and a talented actor, Van Dyke, in his self-titled sitcom, convinced us that he was just like *us*, while doing things we couldn't have hoped to do even half as well. Identification with an actor is a sign of the performer's charm, and in the 1960s everyone wanted to be Dick Van Dyke.

23. **John Fitzgerald Kennedy.** In his day, they called it "charisma," but you might notice that the word "charm" is in there, too. JFK defined a generation during his short time in the world-wide spotlight, and even the very human foibles that were revealed after his death have failed to dim the light of his charm.

24. **Audrey Hepburn.** The most elegant woman on the planet, Hepburn made a career out of playing "regular girls" who were turned into swans. The fact that anyone would even dream of casting her as a Cockney flower girl would seem ludicrous, if she weren't so good at showing us the real human heart beneath the unearthly beauty.

25. **Anthony Hopkins.** The man played a demented, horrible, cannibalistic murderer, and audiences rooted for him to get out of jail. Three times. Why? Because he was just so damn *charming*.

26. **Princess Diana.** We knew everything about her, and we knew nothing about her, but we knew what we wanted to know, and that was enough. When countless millions got up early to watch a wedding on television, it wasn't to see the prince she was marrying—we wanted to see "Shy Di." With her radiant

smile and seeming affinity for people in all walks of life, she
was the princess we all wished for, even if it wasn't what she
would have wished for herself.

27. **Harry Potter.** So he's a fictional character; nobody's perfect.
Harry is the ultimate audience identifier. He's an orphan neg-
lected by his family who discovers he has tremendous powers.
Does he take revenge? No, he simply tries to get by without
being noticed (and fails miserably). And millions around the
world love him for it.

28. **Vanna White.** Job: letter turner. Who would think you could
turn that into a twenty-year career? But Vanna, who in person is one of the most charming people around, became in-
dispensable simply because she was wonderfully likable.
Nobody else could turn those letters the way she does.

29. **Steven Spielberg.** Arguably the most powerful man in entertainment, able to make any film he wants whenever he wants.
Ever seen him interviewed? He's still amazed that they let him
behind the camera. He connects with the audience because he
is always worried about the audience. He feels what we, in the
theaters, feel.

30. **Barbara Walters.** Why do celebrities invite her into their homes,
knowing she's going to make them cry? Sure, they want the
publicity, but they could get that from any of a number of
high-profile interviewers. Walters has made a distinguished
career out of access to the mightiest because she knows how
to charm them into talking to her.

31. **Paul Reiser.** Beginning with a stand-up comedy act and then
acting in a few films and a run-of-the-mill sitcom, Reiser
found his niche with Helen Hunt in *Mad About You*, playing
a man so in love with his wife he can't believe his good fortune.

He found situations that were so universal people would write in asking where the microphone in their bedrooms were hidden.

32. **Sandra Bullock.** Consider a scene in *Miss Congeniality*. Bullock, playing an undercover FBI agent working in a beauty pageant, is unveiled in an evening gown with great makeup and hair—in other words, looking like Sandra Bullock—and everyone is slack-jawed at the amazing transformation. Why? She's able to project a girl-next-door charm while looking like the girl we all *wish* was next door.

33. **Ronald Reagan.** They called him the "Great Communicator." He could explain complex global issues and the general public wouldn't just understand, it would pay attention. His ability to project concern and empathy was legendary.

34. **Ellen DeGeneres.** It would have been hard for anyone else to "come out" as a lesbian on national television. Because she was Ellen, who spoke our language and cared about our issues, we didn't have to blink an eye.

35. **Billy Crystal.** Great comedians find a way to bring the values of the audience to any topic. Crystal can puncture pomposity wherever he finds it (and he's gone as far as Moscow to look) because he's never lost sight of his middle-class New York roots.

36. **Jim Henson.** He could take a piece of felt and make you laugh or cry over it. Because he cared about the story and the characters, Henson created some of the most bizarre and unconventional creatures ever imagined, and made them seem like the monsters next door.

37. **Carol Burnett.** They didn't just trot her out to answer questions from the audience because she was a brilliant stand-up comic—

they did it because she could talk to an audience and relate to them like no one else. She told us what was *really* going on backstage, and made it all seem so wholesome, we loved her for decades.

38. **Alan Alda.** For a generation of Americans, he was the very voice of enlightenment. Voted the man most of America would want to invite over for dinner (more than once), he went from his signature *M*A*S*H* role to a varied cast of characters, and even when he played a bad guy, we expected him to have a very good reason for his villainy.

39. **Harrison Ford.** Stalwart and heroic under all circumstances, when Ford put on that rumpled hat and strapped on his bull-whip, he could have been a frightening figure. But his smile, and the fact that he *wasn't* invincible, made us identify with him all the more.

40. **Jennifer Aniston.** Never afraid to make fun of herself, and the leader in a generation of actresses embodying the "girl-next-door" ideal, Aniston plays women who are not especially glamorous and usually not in extraordinary circumstances because she wants audiences to know she hasn't lost touch. That's charming.

41. **John Goodman.** By all reports one of the nicest guys in Holly-wood, Goodman doesn't let his weight get in his way. He knows that everyone is the star of his own movie, and he shows that everyone deserves to be that star. His decency and humanity are evident even in parts meant to be evil.

42. **Gene Wilder.** Wilder likes to tell a story about Cary Grant saying he admired his performance in *Silver Streak*. Grant told him that that film's formula always works: "You take an average guy, like you or me . . ." and immediately Wilder is saying, "An

average guy? Like me or *Cary Grant?*" But the answer is, yes, Gene, you and Cary Grant. We can see the charming savoir-faire in your eyes.

43. **Jerry Seinfeld.** You ever notice how the really great comedians aren't the ones with an obvious gimmick, but the ones who comment on everyday occurrences? Seinfeld takes the trivial and raises it to universal art, through the power of recognition.

44. **John Wayne.** Nobody ever said he was an actor of great range, but he was great on the range. Wayne was the overachieving protector we all wished we had, who would help us because he knew we were valuable and worth saving. He became an American icon doing it.

45. **Lucille Ball.** Strikingly beautiful, she could have been a dramatic actress in "serious" films. Instead, she decided to black out her teeth, stuff her hat with chocolates, and stumble around on stilts. Because she knew what it was like to look foolish, she made all America laugh.

46. **James Stewart.** Before there was Tom Hanks, there was Jack Lemmon. Before Lemmon, there was Stewart. He embodied the idea of the American male for generations, and was anything but the ideal. He could be petty, obsessed, even livid, but always decent and caring.

47. **Walter Matthau.** Even when he was the shifty double-dealing schemer, he was one of us. Matthau's wit and his tired expression made him an audience favorite, because he never took anything—including himself—too seriously.

48. **Katharine Hepburn.** If Audrey was the princess, Katharine was the queen. Never worried about being taken down a peg, Hepburn's long and illustrious career was all about realizing what life was all about. Often, she started with one idea and ended

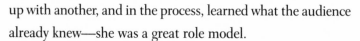

up with another, and in the process, learned what the audience already knew—she was a great role model.

49. **Julia Roberts.** Who else could make a movie about a prostitute and win America's hearts? Roberts never plays the gorgeous glamour queen—she's always a girl who could use a break or a better man—but the entire audience can see the *Pretty Woman* within.

50. **Abraham Lincoln.** The man who once said, "If I was two-faced, would I be using this one?" had more on his mind than most presidents would ever be burdened with, yet he kept his wit about him and solidly steered the country through its most trying time. With a gentle, self-deprecating sense of humor and a fierce intellect, Lincoln was charming and rose to the very top.

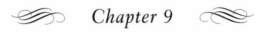

Chapter 9

Hollywood Charm

Hollywood, it has been noted, is not an easy place to live or work. The competition is as fierce as it gets on this planet, the stakes are higher than almost anywhere else, and the tension—which is always present—can be cut with a knife.

For those who believe that Los Angeles is a city where dreams really do come true, let me assure you they do—about 0.0001 percent of the time. I have worked in the entertainment industry in Hollywood for more than twenty years, and I can tell you that the rest of the time, this town is tough, brutal, and about as much the opposite of charming as you can get.

What's interesting, though, is that quite often, it is the person who is charming, who has the social skills, and takes the time to make sure he or she does the things that endear us to others, who makes it up the ladder in the corporate side of the business. The "talent" who takes the time to be charming will, as the list in the last chapter may illustrate, stand out from the crowd and make an impression that will create a career. Quite often, that career is one that endures.

Hollywood isn't always an easy place to be charming, but as the song about another city says, if you can make it here, you can make it anywhere. All it takes is talent, and a little charm. Okay, a *lot* of charm.

Remember that in Hollywood "personality" refers both to a human being and to the qualities he or she possesses. In fact, "personality" can be a job in the entertainment industry—they're the people in show business who don't act or dance or sing or tell jokes, but they're famous anyway.

"Hollywood," you should realize, is not a particular piece of real estate, although it is a section of Los Angeles (and one where remarkably little related to the film industry happens these days). It is, rather, a state of mind, and shorthand for the entertainment industry, which encompasses movies, television, and to some extent radio and recording. Hollywood, then, is a particular thing that each of us can recognize, but none of us can precisely define.

Much like charm.

Here are the steps toward making a success of yourself in Hollywood:

1. **Have some talent.** Keep in mind, it doesn't have to be a *creative* talent. Yes, film directors, actors, writers, and other creative people are essential to the Hollywood we all know, but they are not the entire industry. If there were no one with the talent to produce films, to recognize creativity, to finance the enterprise, and to make the business profitable, being the most creative person on the planet wouldn't guarantee success.

2. **Persist.** There are some amazingly talented writers, actors, directors, and artists working in Hollywood—as waiters, counter help, executive assistants, word processors, and

delivery personnel. This is true for two reasons—first, because some of these people don't have the drive or stamina to make it, and have dropped out of the Hollywood game, and second, because the rest have to pay the bills while persisting through all types of adversity. Charm is an asset, but it won't help if you give up at the first rejection.

3. **Network.** If the saying "it's not what you know; it's *who* you know" is true anywhere in this world, that place is Hollywood. The job market is so tight, and there are so many applicants, that just being perfect for the job isn't enough—you have to know *somebody*. This is going to be an area where charm is absolutely invaluable. You can't network if nobody wants to talk to you.

4. **Network more.** It can't be emphasized enough. Finding work in Hollywood is like finding a nugget of gold in a well-picked stream. It's possible, but it's not likely, and it sure as heck isn't easy. Get to know more people in town who are in the business, or know people in the business, and you have a much better chance of finding that door open just a crack.

5. **Learn your craft.** It doesn't do any good to know anybody if you can't back up your claims with the ability to do the job. While you're out there looking for work and meeting the up-and-comers, you have to be honing your talents so that when the chance comes, you can leap at it.

6. **Keep eating.** You have to earn a living while you're still on this side of fame and fortune. Work at something to pay the bills, and see that as an opportunity as well. Remember the waiter who painted watercolors—those who are charming at their "day jobs" will have a better chance of moving on to their desired careers.

7. **Practice, practice, practice.** This refers to two things: first, you must practice the art or craft you hope to make a career; second, you have to keep your charming skills sharp and ready, and there is no better way to do that than by practicing them at every possible turn.

8. **Did I mention networking?**

Now, the vast majority of those who read this book will be wondering exactly why they're learning the skills necessary to survive in Hollywood. Because about 98 percent of those reading this book have *no* intention of heading to Los Angeles to pursue a career in the entertainment industry. Well, there are two reasons: Hollywood, first of all, is perhaps the most extreme example of a place where business competition is going to be fierce and constant. Everyone understands the stakes involved, and as it has been observed on more than one occasion, in their minds, everyone is in two businesses: their own and show business.

Second, all of the above steps to success in the entertainment industry involve the use of charm. By using them as clear examples, which can show the way to success in *your* business, you can have a better picture of why and how charm can be the incredibly valuable tool I've been telling you it is.

Think of the eight steps. *Have some talent.* There is no sense in entering a business for which you have no aptitude whatsoever. Granted, sometimes you don't know how much aptitude you have until you try out a skill, but after a short period of time, those with no talent for the work (and worse, no interest in it) will quickly be revealed, both to themselves and to their employers. Try everything you think might be right for you, but stick with a field that best strikes your fancy and for which you have a discernible flair. You'll be more charming to the people with whom you work and the ones *for* whom you work—the clients or customers. Climbing the ladder will be that much easier.

Persist. Nothing worthwhile was every accomplished easily. Okay, maybe it was easy to invent the Frisbee, but making it a household name and a worldwide astounding success was the result of inspiration, planning, and very, very hard work. Things are going to get tough, no matter what business you happen to be in. You have to have the guts (and the charm) to stick it out. The more charming in this group will, strikingly, need it less, since there will be a certain amount of goodwill engendered simply by being charming, so even though things *will* get tough, they might not be as tough, or last as long.

Network, and network more. Here's where charm is really at the forefront. There are personal connections in every business (and no, I don't mean dating situations or romances, although they do happen) —you're going to be recommended or not based to a large extent on the type of impression you make, both in business and social situations related to business. If you flex your charm muscles, and make yourself well liked within the small, closed community that is your field, you will definitely be more successful—it's as simple as that.

Learn your craft. Craft is the encoded rule of the industry you're in, and every business has it. It's one thing to know how to do some-thing—it's quite something else to know how to do it *well*. Charm can get you in the door, but it won't make a sale for you. Being the best at what you do will. Charm also comes into play in the area of mentors and teachers, those who already know how to be the best at what you hope to be. The more charming you are, the more likely they'll be willing to share with you what they know.

Keep eating. Every business has its "salad days" period. Charm helps speed the process between hourly wage earner and career professional. Keep at your first or entry level job, doing it in the most charming way possible, to best achieve your goal—leaving that job and moving on to the next. Charm, with the public and with co-workers and employers, will go a very long way toward helping you move up the ladder.

Practice, practice, practice. Mostly, practice your charm. Yes, get good at what you do, that's terribly important, but charm is a skill that can be helpful in every aspect of life, and something that should be practiced at every possible opportunity. Charm is the special skill that will make you stand out. The more you practice it, the more natural and effortless it will become. And that, as we have proven, can go a long way toward helping you realize your business goals, and your personal ones as well.

Did I mention networking? There's no replacement for human contact in business—simply put, the people who like you are going to be more likely to hire you or recommend you. Getting to know as many people as you can in any field—and getting them to like you—is essential. Not important—*essential*.

In the *real* Hollywood, however, charm is practiced by the most adept people on the planet. This is the Major Leagues of Charm, and you'd be amazed how good some people are at it. But you'd be *more* amazed at how *bad* others manage to be.

Here's the secret: you can rest assured that the bitchiest, the rudest, the most obnoxious of the divas and prima donnas in Holly-wood were as charming and reasonable as can be—when they were just starting out. The problem is that once they achieved an unexpected (to everyone but them) level of success, once they had charmed their way to the top, they felt it was acceptable to "drop the act" and forget about the common courtesies and outright people-pleasing skills that make up charm, and helped them along the way.

You see this quite a bit in the entertainment business. Performers especially (although executives and businesspeople are offenders at least as often in this way) start to "believe their own press" after they are stars, and no longer feel it necessary to empathize with others, listen to their troubles, or offer help or a shoulder to cry on—or even a thank-you note.

This is, to a certain extent, understandable. The biggest stars (and even lesser ones, if the truth be known) in entertainment are surrounded by people who think their jobs will be in jeopardy if they tell them something other than what they want to hear. So everything a star hears about himself is positive and complimentary. No one would *ever* have the nerve to point out that a big star is being rude. After a while, the idea that such a thing is *possible* leaves stars' minds. They act accordingly.

But the ones who stay focused, keep their feet on the ground, and remain *charming*—people such as Linda Evans, Tom Hanks, and Sherry Lansing—are the ones whose careers tend to last longer, and whose work continues to be at the higher level set when the entertainer began.

The dirty truth of the matter is that when someone gets "too big" and loses the desire (and hence, the ability) to charm, Hollywood enjoys nothing better than seeing him fall, and hard. No one will be nearby with a net, and nobody will offer a hand to pick that person back up off the ground. There are countless examples of stars who burned out, and in the cases where the charm was no longer a factor, there are very few stories of comebacks.

Consider, however, someone like John Travolta, whose star has risen (and fallen, it must be said) a few times. Without charm, without the desire and the ability to be *nice* to people, there would have been no second chance, let alone a third. Travolta might have been that guy who was a movie star for a couple of years after *Welcome Back, Kotter*. Instead, he is an enduring talent who continues to charm audiences and colleagues to this day.

Others, whose names I won't mention, have not been so lucky. They have, instead, charmed their way to the bottom, by forgetting the necessity of charm.

Does this mean that anyone who sends thank-you notes and responds to invitations promptly can be a huge movie star? Of course not. There has to be a combination of talent, drive, and luck to begin with. And some without charm will certainly reach the top—the gossip columns are loaded with such stories of petty and rude behavior.

But, those who *do* practice charm in Hollywood tend to rise higher and stay there longer than those who don't. It's a simple rule of mathematics—watch the ones who are in the public's eye for decades, not years. Charming? Almost without question. Yes, there are exceptions, but they are exactly that—exceptions, because the majority of those who make it to the top learned long ago that they could use something they had naturally or learned along the way to help them—charm.

Hollywood is as tough a town as I have ever seen, but when someone uses charm, you can see the whole city open its eyes and take notice. Every business, don't forget, is a small town, and news gets around quickly—more quickly today than ever before. And remember, also, that charm makes an impression. That information will be disseminated around your business just as quickly.

Those who are charming, therefore, are going to get that reputation, and those who *continue* to be charming will be able to keep it.

In this town, that is a very important quality.

$\ggg$ *Chapter 10* $\lll$

The Most Charming Man Ever

In recorded history, there have been people who used their natural charm to seduce the opposite sex, to acquire great riches, to gain fame or power. There have been people who used their charm as a weapon, and those who used it as a salve. Some incredibly successful people used charm to convince others of their position on politics, business, or achievement.

But there has never, *ever* been anyone more charming than Cary Grant.

The absolute template for charm in the twentieth century, Cary Grant wasn't the most versatile actor who ever lived, although his talents were often underrated. He was not skilled in the way that a contemporary like Spencer Tracy was; he was not lusted after in the same way as other male leads like Clark Gable or Errol Flynn were (although many women—and men—pined for Grant). He was nominated once for an Academy Award, and lost. It wasn't until much later, decades after he retired, that Grant was awarded an honorary Oscar for his enduring legacy and the breadth and length of his career.

But my goodness, he was charming.

Cary Grant defined charm from the 1930s until the 1970s, an unprecedented career during which he was the charmer against whom all others were measured—and found lacking. Tony Curtis did an impression of Grant in *Some Like It Hot* simply to convey a precise image of charm; no other explanation was necessary. The imitation won him Marilyn Monroe, after all. As late as the mid 1970s, Burt Reynolds did a Grant impression in another film, for the same purpose. It wasn't necessary to explain that this character was trying to be charming—it was obvious, because he was trying to be Cary Grant.

Late into his career, Grant was seen as the pinnacle of grace and charm, luring much younger costars such as Audrey Hepburn, Eva Marie Saint, and Grace Kelly. The difference in age was never a problem for him or his leading ladies, and again the message was clear: Who wouldn't want Cary Grant?

Men wanted desperately to be like Grant, because it would mean that women would find them irresistible. Women wanted to find someone like Grant, and found most other men lacking by comparison. Truly, if there were a picture in the dictionary next to the word "charming," even today it would be a photograph of Cary Grant.

While he does not fit the same profile as today's male superstars, measuring Grant's impact on American culture (and indeed, popular culture around the world) would be impossible. He was more than an actor. He was an icon, an example. Grant, simply speaking, was charm.

How did he do it? Cary Grant began life as Archie Leach in Bristol, England, in 1904. After a rough childhood, during which his mother was committed to a mental institution by his alcoholic father, Archie gravitated toward the theater, beginning as an acrobat in a traveling troupe, and eventually ending up in films as early as 1931.

Because of his chiseled good looks, Grant was initially cast as the "juvenile," or male love interest, in a number of films, including a few appearances with Mae West during which the grande dame did little more than leer at the handsome young man in her presence and request that he "come up some time and see me."

It didn't take long for the Cary Grant persona to crystallize, though. Grant polished his image to a fine sheen in films like *Mr. Lucky, The Philadelphia Story, His Girl Friday,* and Alfred Hitchcock's *Suspicion*. He was always tall and handsome, he always had the clipped accent that was eventually construed as "upper class," and he was never anything other than courteous.

In short, Cary Grant was always charming.

How did this manifest itself in his public persona? On-screen, Grant was always fair, always listened to the women he was wooing, dressed elegantly (even when he didn't need to), and was the very picture of consideration and courtesy. Under the most dire circumstances, he would not be nasty. Given every opportunity to revolt against Katharine Hepburn in *Bringing Up Baby* (1938), he was always gracious, politely asked her to stop doing what she was doing, and fell in love with her even as she refused to do so.

In *North by Northwest* (1959), Grant explains his philosophy of romance to Eva Marie Saint: "Every time I meet an attractive woman, I have to pretend I have no interest in making love to her," he says. Why? "She might find the idea objectionable." Now, *that's* polite.

How did that help Grant rise to the top of his profession? Being the very definition of charm was an enormous asset to him. Cary Grant guaranteed box office success for decades, because audiences (chiefly women) wanted to see him being charming, and men wanted to pretend that they could be as smooth, as cool, and as well received as Grant presented himself on-screen.

When Alfred Hitchcock wanted Grant to portray a murderer in *Suspicion* (1941), the studio wouldn't allow it, feeling audiences would reject the idea of such a charming man being capable of killing his wife. The ending of the film was rewritten to have the wife's suspicions be unfounded. Public opinion prevailed, and Grant's image was cemented. He could never play a cold-blooded killer.

Offscreen, Grant's image was always one of a polite, accessible, friendly man. Despite rumors about his personal life, Grant was never combative with the press, answered questions, and made himself available to fans. He married five times, but none of his ex-wives had anything negative to say about him.

Why was Cary Grant so convincing in the role he chose to play? Because he had trained himself, from a very early age, to understand what other people wanted from him, and to deliver it whenever it was possible. Once his public face was established in the 1930s, he very rarely tried to break free of the image. Grant made sure that if he went out on a limb, as he did with a film called *Crisis* (1950) in which he played a brilliant brain surgeon, that he followed it up with something familiar, like *Operation Pacific* (1951), and not long after, a Hitchcock role in *To Catch a Thief* (1954), in which he seduced Grace Kelly almost against his own will.

In his personal life, Grant was not as smooth as he wanted to be. None of his marriages lasted longer than ten years, and he had only one child, a daughter with Dyan Cannon, whom he married when he was close to sixty. Grant reportedly was given to periods of depression and felt trapped by the character he had created to play all his life.

Outwardly, however, none of that showed. Grant was a consummate professional when on a movie set, by all accounts did not require special treatment, which often would be demanded by a star of his caliber, and was not given to temper tantrums involving his work. He charmed one and all on the set, and rarely was a negative word spoken about Cary Grant in Hollywood.

The word most often used to label him, in fact, was "gentleman." That is a compliment not often heard in the grating times we now inhabit, but it was important to understanding Cary Grant. There were gentlemen in other movies, and there were men arguably as good-looking as Archie Leach, but Cary Grant was a creature unto himself. Even playing a Cockney who got into gang trouble in *None But the Lonely Heart* (1944), he was never mean or uncouth; playing a gambler in *Mr. Lucky* (1943), he meant to scam a lovely lady out of her money, but he couldn't bring himself to do it. In *Charade* (1965), there is every reason for Audrey Hepburn to believe that Grant is a vicious killer out to steal her money and take her life. Yet, given tons of evidence against him, she trusts him over the voice of authority, mostly because he is Cary Grant, and when she asks why she should believe him, he grins and says, "I can't think of one reason why you should."

The lesson of Cary Grant to be learned while you're charming your way to the top is that someone who personified all the attributes we consider charming might have been a personally conflicted, flawed man, but the face he showed to those he wanted to charm was one of pure ingratiating attention. He always wanted to talk about you, not about himself. He wanted to help you, not worry about his own problems. Even when confronted with spies out to assassinate him, agents betraying him and the police chasing him all over the country in *North by Northwest*, Cary Grant stopped and faced the music when the woman he'd come to love was in danger. It would have been just as easy to extricate himself from the plot and go home, but he went so far as to become a target because someone else needed help.

When trying to seduce women (which he often did in his films), Grant was all attention, talking about their needs and feelings. He gave out little information about his own life, and always steered the conversation back to the woman. In *Indiscreet* (1958), he pretended to be married so Ingrid Bergman would think they were having an illicit affair and he couldn't marry her. Grant kept insisting that Bergman tell him more about her, so he could stop talking about himself (he didn't want to betray his lie). But he kept his secret even after deciding he was in love with Bergman, until she uncovered it herself. Even when he was trying to be a cad, Grant could charm the estimable Ms. Bergman into falling in love with him.

Grant could charm men, as well. At the beginning of *North by Northwest*, a film that played heavily on Grant's well-established persona, Grant cheats another man out of a cab on Madison Avenue in New York by lying that his secretary is "a very sick woman" and needs the car. When his secretary scolds him for lying to the man, Grant tells her that he made the man "feel like a good Samaritan. Remember, Maggie, in the world of advertising, there is no such thing as a lie; there is only the expedient exaggeration." It's even possible the man who gave up his cab knew that Grant was lying, and didn't care. After all, such a charming man must have needed the cab desperately to cheat his way into it like that.

In his action roles like *Gunga Din* (1939) and *Charade*, Grant made male audience members comfortable by not being larger than life and making them feel inferior; on the contrary, Grant played the roles with flaws, clumsiness, and difficulties, to better help them feel they could easily do the same things as the man on the screen, perhaps better.

The on-screen persona Grant cultivated is very important, because it is the largest piece of the overall character he created to show the outside world, and therefore became the way he was measured by the public, which found him to be the King of Charm. In his films, Grant was one of the actors who played variations on the same role. It was as if Archie Leach were acting in a series of movies about the same character, someone named Cary Grant. Through this, Grant spoke the same way, moved the same way, and conveyed emotion with the same mannerisms. But his performances did vary to serve the story. Over-the-top comedies, such as *Arsenic and Old Lace* (1944) or *Mr. Blandings Builds His Dream House* (1948), required over-the-top characterizations, and Grant provided them. For more serious films, like *Penny Serenade* (1941) or *None But the Lonely Heart*, he played the same general character, but in a more subdued mode.

Grant's gift was that of intuition; he knew instinctively what would be required to make another person (or many other people) feel important, and therefore feel positively about the person who had provided that emotion. He played the part of Cary Grant seamlessly for sixty years, and made it a virtual trademark of charm and grace.

Unlike someone like Fred Astaire, a contemporary who also appeared frequently in tuxedo and moved with incredible grace and elegance, Grant was an approachable ideal, the kind of persona that invited audiences to sit down and talk, not to stand back and admire. That is extremely important in the business of charming your way to the top; if someone merely admires your skills and talents, that person is more likely to envy you than to feel charmed. Making the other person feel comfortable is key. Instead of standing back and watching you go through your paces, the other person should feel that he has been the object of most of the attention. People love the sound of their own names, and they want to feel that you consider them important. Cary Grant had the ability, even with his impressive physical and artistic gifts, to project the image of a "regular guy" who would be happy to sit down and listen to your life story, rather than bore you with his own.

Grant's offscreen life was not as well orchestrated as his career. He was rumored to be bisexual, and although he denied the rumors later in his life, the rumors persisted and were tied to the idea that Cary Grant, of all people, couldn't make himself happy by falling in love. Stories surfaced that Grant had tried LSD, was such a perfectionist about himself that he couldn't ever be satisfied with any accomplishment of his own, and was never happy with any of his wives, yearning instead for costars like Sophia Loren.

These stories, however, were rarely printed in the mainstream press. Grant's public face was always that of the Cary Grant character, since he was afraid that people wouldn't take as readily to Archie Leach. He was very careful to protect the Grant image, and in his last years, he toured the country cultivating the image anew, telling stories of his career and talking about being Cary Grant.

While Grant was not a businessman per se, he was adept at getting what he felt was his due in his profession. When the roles he was being offered were no longer what he felt were right for him, Grant left Paramount Pictures in 1937 and did not sign a contract with another studio; he was one of the first actors to operate as a "free agent," able to choose his own roles and negotiate his own salary.

But no matter how tough a businessman he could be, Grant was always spoken of with affection and respect in Hollywood. His charm had served him well; Grant knew the ultimate lesson of charming your way to the top: how to say "no" to someone and still have him or her like you afterward.

That is no small feat. There isn't a person alive who likes to be told he can't have what he wants, and telling someone "no" in any context (personal, professional, familial) can be a very difficult task indeed. Learning how to do so with charm is central to the ability to rise within a bureaucracy or business structure while maintaining respect from one's peers.

Cary Grant knew how to do that, but then, Cary Grant knew how to do everything, or at least that is what we, the audience, believed. He was accessible, but larger than life; he was the kind of person we all wished we could be.

Once, when an interviewer suggested that "everybody would like to be Cary Grant," the man himself countered, "so would I."

Now, that's charming.

Chapter 11

The Dark Side of Charm

Charm has a dark side.

It is one thing to define charm by the good feeling it instills in us, and that is usually the easy definition. It is often accurate, but not always.

There are many examples of people who use charm to achieve ends that are not at all charming. Many businesspeople are extremely charming at the job interview, and then ruthless, belligerent, and mean-spirited once you're hired.

Reggie Jackson remembered being "courted" by George Steinbrenner III when Jackson was a free agent in the winter of 1976. Steinbrenner brought Jackson to New York, took him out to dinner, introduced him to powerful and famous people, and eventually, Reggie signed a five-year contract to play for Steinbrenner's New York Yankees.

That contract would become five tumultuous years during which the star player; his team manager, Billy Martin; and Steinbrenner, the team owner, would often clash, argue, sometimes come within a hairsbreadth of violence, and never stay out of the bright light that is the media focus in New York. But what Jackson remembered years later was how charming Steinbrenner had been in the beginning.

Another example might be Roseanne Barr, who was in a very powerful position in Hollywood in the late 1980s and early 1990s, due to her extremely successful sitcom, *Roseanne*. By all reports difficult, sometimes combative, and often vulgar, Barr alienated many members of the team with whom she created the show, including some of the executive producers and network executives who had given her the chance to perform on television in the first place.

Why did they put up with this kind of behavior? Because Barr was talented and (mostly) because the ratings were very high. It could be argued, too, that the ratings remained high, that people watched the show week after week, because Barr had managed, through the persona she created and cultivated, to charm mass audiences. They tuned in because they believed in her—she was one of them. In other words, Roseanne made much of America feel that she understood its problems and sympathized. That is a strong definition of charm, even if it was not practiced one-on-one, but projected to the masses as a whole.

Still, a baseball team owner who isn't always nice to his employees or a television actress who can be obnoxious in personal relationships and difficult professionally are minor examples. The dark side of charm has a much more frightening and cautionary tale to tell.

The Worst Person Ever?

By almost every yardstick imaginable the most evil man of the twentieth century, Adolph Hitler set new standards for behavior that was unconscionable in every possible way. His actions were, in any reasonable person's estimation, absolutely, unimaginably horrific.

Still, if we are examining how people rise to positions of power and influence, we have to at least consider how such a man, with a message of hate and intolerance, of murder and atrocities, could possible have risen to so high and, in a critical time in the world's history, come within a very narrow margin of gaining control over most of the planet.

Therefore, the question must be asked: Was Hitler charming?

A few words of disclaimer before we begin to examine this issue. I am not a historian. The influences and incidents that had to come together in order for this monster to gain control of a nation are complex and myriad; I do not claim to encompass them all in my argument. We are examining this moment in history strictly from the standpoint of how charm is used, and abused. And even in that context, we are discussing the subject strictly within our own definition of charm. I would not for a millisecond claim that Hitler was a nice guy or someone to emulate in your attempt to charm your way to the top. On the contrary, I think we need to examine his tactics as an example of how such a thing can go horribly wrong and create a catastrophe unheard of in all of history. If for no other reason, we should consider this question to make absolutely certain we can recognize the techniques used and the signs they indicate, so that no one like Hitler ever rises to power again.

That said, let's examine our initial question: Was Adolf Hitler charming?

First, let's recall our very specific definition of charm. It is the art and the craft of convincing the other person that you care about his concerns. That's basic and simple, and doesn't really encompass every aspect of what charm is, but it is the best working definition we have available right now, and it can certainly help us determine what the answer to our question should be.

The clerk at the shoe store is charming if she makes us believe that she is concerned about our fallen arches and pinched toes. The actor is charming if he can tap into the emotion in us that makes us relate to the character he plays (in other words, if he makes us believe that is *us* up there on the screen). The athlete is charming is he excels at something we could never do, and is then humble about it and gives all the credit for the achievement to his teammates and "hard work."

Politicians are charming when they make us believe that they are concerned about the same things that we are concerned about, *and that they have a way to make those things better.*

When George H. W. Bush won the 1988 presidential election, it was largely because he convinced Americans that they could trust him in one area—taxes—about which they were most concerned. His son's victory in 2000 was at least partially attributable to his promise to cut taxes again. When Bill Clinton won in 1992, he convinced the public that he could "feel their pain" in a sluggish economy, and that he had plans that would make that pain go away.

Let's look, then, at the Germany into which Adolf Hitler rose to power in the 1920s and 1930s. Beaten in World War I, its economy was a shambles and its people were defeated and frustrated. Unable to change the conditions around them, the Germans were open to any suggestion of a solution by someone who understood what they were going through and promised to restore their dignity.

At that moment, Hitler's message—that the current troubles could be overcome, that Germany could indeed become proud and dominant again, and that the current conditions were not the fault of the general populace—were all attractive to the average German during this period. It was that initial message, the Nazi equivalent of "I feel your pain," that was first heard in the *biergartens* and plazas of the average German town.

Desperate times may call for desperate measures, but they also tend to promote rash decisions. In this tragic case, the need of the German people to escape their dire circumstances and feel dignity and power again was twisted by a madman into justification for racism, genocide, and world war. But how did it happen? How were so many people misled so hideously and completely? In retrospect, it seems impossible, but it happened. How can we explain this?

Because he made them believe, and because he lied.

By telling the population that he understood their troubles, and that he could not only alleviate but also solve their problems—and by giving them a number of convenient scapegoats upon which to blame those problems—Hitler managed to convince huge numbers of people that the impossibly sick, twisted solution he proposed was the proper way to proceed. Of course, the most distasteful details of Hitler's plan, the horrible genocide and destructive megalomania his actions would eventually become, were not part of his initial message. Even people in the direst of circumstances would not have agreed to those plans had they been made public and proposed in a referendum. At first, the message was simply that Germany could be saved and its dignity restored. That was especially persuasive to a proud people who had been humiliated and beaten in a war relatively recently.

People who are hungry for good news would latch on to this type of message. They would believe the messenger because he brought the message they wanted. The details of that message wouldn't have to be clear and they wouldn't have to be made public. The promise would be enough.

Is this charm? It is *part* of charm, but not the quality in and of itself. In addition, there would have to be an emotional connection, something that convinced the populace that Hitler didn't just believe what he said, but that he *felt* the way that they felt.

In Germany during the rise of National Socialism, a good percentage of the populace was angry. The lives of many people had taken a severe downturn, for reasons that they saw as anything but their own doing. They wanted to express that anger, to let it out and to direct it at someone other than themselves. And when he spoke to the masses, Hitler vented that anger—he provided an outlet for the emotion they were feeling, and made it *acceptable* and *understandable*.

It is one thing to release emotion and help people express what they are feeling. It is something else entirely to make that emotion an excuse to eschew responsibility and blame every ill on other elements of society.

Can we call this charm? Can we say that in telling the people what they wanted to hear, and thereby creating a racist, anti-Semitic culture that would plunge the world into chaos, that Hitler was charming the majority of the German people? It's not as much a stretch as it might seem.

Let's examine what tactics were being used here. A political candidate (and eventually, political leader) of a country told the vast majority of voters in his country that they weren't at fault for the awful conditions they were experiencing. He told them—and showed them through his tone and actions—that he could empathize with their plight, that he had come from the same humble beginnings as many of them, and that he could certainly understand what they were going through. "I understand," he told them. "I sympathize, and I know your lives can, and should, be better. I have a plan to help."

And he gave them someone (in fact, many groups) to blame, people who were different and frightening, and who appeared to be profiting from the plight of the "average German."

If you claim long enough to be a man of the people and you give the people the message they're desperate to hear—*if, in other words, you tell the people that you care about their problems*, your message will not only be perceived as important and worthwhile.

It will be charming.

Charming, remember, doesn't have to be Cary Grant. It doesn't have to be *Hugh* Grant. It is simply the quality that makes us trust someone enough to buy his product, vote for his party, watch his movie, root for his team, or buy him dinner.

One quality that is almost always mentioned in connection with a successful political leader (and many successful businesspeople, as well) is the ability to make you believe that while you are in that person's presence, she is concentrating fervently on *you*, for no matter how short a period of time. These people make you believe that you are the most important person in their world, even if it's only for a moment. And that is about as practical an example of charm as can be imagined.

If a leader can translate that quality into the ability to make a huge crowd, a television audience, or the whole country feel the same way (and in order to become a successful political leader, it is likely such a person can do just that), they have an enormous amount of power. Facts, plans, and policies might convince the voters' brains, but emotions rule their hearts, and are both more deeply trusted and easier to manipulate. This appeal is the stuff of tremendous loyalty and equally huge danger.

The rise and fall of Adolf Hitler is a cautionary tale in virtually every context. It teaches against believing an opportunist who tells you what you want to hear against all logic. It warns against blaming large social ills on a segment of the population. It makes a very strong case for keeping a very close eye on all political leaders, no matter how popular they may be.

It also reveals the dark side of charm, and how dangerous that quality can be under the right (or wrong) circumstances.

Naturally, this is the most extreme example of charm's danger. In more mundane circumstances, the quality of charm might be used by an unscrupulous business associate or a customer who tries to manipulate your company away from the course it has been following. It would be less dangerous to society, but it would still be damaging to you.

As you cultivate your own charm, keep in mind too that it should be used responsibly. That doesn't mean you always have to be a doormat; you're not required to give in to your competition or your colleagues when their actions go against your own interests. But it does mean that you shouldn't try to charm people into doing something that will do them harm, and you shouldn't present false charm that leads to an impression or a promise you can't deliver.

You are constantly practicing the activities that will be seen as charming, as you should. You should be charming to as many people as you can in the course of an average day—the florist, the parking attendant, your assistant, your competitor. But make sure that the charm you're practicing is the right kind—you're not lying, you can't make promises you know you won't keep. It is not charming to renege on agreements or to bait and switch, to seem to offer something while in truth, you're either offering something else or nothing at all.

Cary Grant wouldn't lie to get what he wanted—he'd be witty, he'd be urbane, he'd even indulge in the odd "expedient exaggeration," but he wouldn't lie. Cary Grant wouldn't claim to have qualities or gifts he didn't actually possess. He wouldn't make promises he knew were impossible to keep.

While we all can't reach the heights of charm that Mr. Grant managed (and which, in fact, no one else has managed since), we can strive for them. We can *try* to be Cary Grant, all the while knowing it's impossible for us to reach that level. It is definitely better to try for an ideal we know we won't achieve than to settle for a mediocrity we know we can.

On the dark side of charm there is a man who would use any means to achieve what he wanted, who would tell anyone and everyone exactly what they wanted to hear whether it was the truth or not, who would use the natural wariness we all possess about those who are different in some way to foster anger and resentment from which he would benefit. This man would use his own charm to convince those with whom he met personally that his negative reputation was a mistake, even a terrible lie concocted by his enemies, and then fulfill that reputation and more with his deeds when no one was paying attention. He would use the cutthroat approach to charm, smiling to someone's face while plotting his demise, and he would convince everyone within earshot that it was the right thing to do.

And quite frankly, I think we've mentioned that man's name enough for one book.

Chapter 12

Exceptions That Prove the Rule

There are people who are ultrasuccessful, who head huge companies, star in megabudget movies, make millions of dollars, and become household names, and are *not* charming. They don't possess an ounce of charisma, are rude and inconsiderate to those around them, regularly treat people they don't know badly, and have reputations that are, to say the least, not incredibly complimentary.

Does this mean that charm *isn't* important to success? Has everything we've been talking about been based on a false premise?

Well, let's think about that. When you were in school, did you know someone who never seemed to study, who didn't even know where the textbook was, let alone what was written inside? Someone who seemed to daydream through class and ignore the teacher?

Sometimes, that was also the person in class who got the best grades, though, wasn't it? And sometimes, that was the person who got into the best college and got the best job after graduation.

Does that mean that studying isn't important for a good education?

Charm is a tool and an attribute that can be beneficial to anyone who wants to succeed in any business or personal endeavor. But it's not the *only* tool or the *only* attribute, and occasionally, there will be a person who manages to succeed in spite of being utterly without charm. That doesn't mean charm is unimportant; it simply means that whatever other talents or qualities that person possesses were enough to overcome the absence of charm.

They'd still be better off cultivating their own ability to be charming, in my opinion. Remember the case of the Hollywood executive I mentioned previously? People might fear you and do your bidding when you're at the top, but if you start to slip and you lack charm, don't be surprised if they watch with glee when you fall.

But how does this happen? How can someone who isn't nice to people, who lacks any sense of courtesy and doesn't make others feel he is in touch with their concerns, succeed at *anything* that involves other people? Most of us aren't born wealthy; plenty of non-charming executives started with very little, and acted this way while they were ascending the ladder. Why didn't the lack of charm deter them from success?

Remember, we're not talking here about people who can *fake* charm. These are not smooth operators who can give the impression that they're concerned for your welfare and then act in ways that are only beneficial to themselves. We're talking in this case about people who never had any charm, and couldn't disguise the fact that they lacked it. These are people who were rude and inconsiderate from the start, and never made the smallest attempt to conceal that fact.

So how can that be? Why would anyone lend a helping hand to someone who acts in such a fashion? And doesn't everyone who is enormously successful need help from others along the way?

There's a cold, hard fact to be faced here. Sometimes, people who are rude and coarse are also enormously *talented*. This may not seem fair, but it is true, and those talents are going to be recognized and needed by various industries. The people who possess them are going to be in demand, no matter what kind of behavior they exhibit, because their talents will make them productive and, for companies, profitable. In other words, they will be valuable no matter what kind of people they happen to be.

Consider the success Dennis Rodman had with the Chicago Bulls of Michael Jordan and Scottie Pippen. Rodman was considered outrageous, even obnoxious, by many of the fans and the owners of the team—even by his teammates at times. But because he was extremely talented, and could produce the kind of results the Bulls needed at the time, his unorthodox behavior was tolerated by all. Once those skills started to erode, however, it was not long before Rodman was headed out of town, and eventually out of the game.

In the entertainment industry, I have worked with a number of people who were not the least bit courteous—forget charming. They were usually people (and this is not referring strictly to "talent," such as actors or directors, but to executives and businesspeople as well) who were at the top of their game and felt they could lord their power over everyone else. They made no effort to hide their bad behavior, and never acknowledged those who worked for them, other than to throw a tantrum when something was not done properly.

I've dealt with "difficult" performers who demanded so many concessions in their contracts that promoters and producers had to forego any common sense and act in accordance of the unusual—some would say "silly"—demands in order to complete the production.

The legendary provision in a band's contract that only a certain color of M&M™s could be included in backstage candy dishes is an example of such a case. While the band members insisted it was written in "just to see if anyone was reading the contract," the fact was that some poor (probably underpaid) employee of the promoter had to weed out the offending candies, and probably would not have used the term "charming" to allude to that band ever again.

There have been reports of performers who demanded that no one on the set of their videos look directly at them. There have been divas who wouldn't come out of the dressing room until an offending plant was moved off the set. There have been actors who have had the director fired for suggesting they might be demanding too many close-ups. There have been executives (in every industry) who abused and humiliated their assistants until the underlings were neurotic, shattered individuals.

Yet, all the people described above had risen to heights of power and influence in their professions. Some were unusually talented, but others merely knew the ins and outs of the business well enough to be useful—that's the key. People who can demonstrate their ability to make a profit for the company will find a way to rise to the top, but without charm, the odds that they'll stay there long are not good.

Beyond talent, there is a knowledge of business—and particularly, of the industry in which one works—that can sometimes compensate for a lack of charm. Again, this is an example of making yourself useful to a specific business or a specific company, and it is effective if you are focused enough to devote yourself to the study of that business and nothing else. An encyclopedic knowledge of the way the industry operates will become a kind of talent, and it will be a salient point when trying to rise within an industry. But if you are capable of that kind of total focus, you can surely learn to develop charm, as well, and have even more powerful tools at your disposal.

By all accounts, Thomas A. Edison was not an easy man to work for. Moody, driven, consumed with the idea that a new invention should be produced practically on a weekly basis, Edison did not bother, when working in his lab, to employ much charm, no matter what Spencer Tracy might have done in the movie *Edison, the Man*. While Edison was far from an ogre, he was single-minded, and tended to let his work overcome him, even including sleeping quarters for himself in his company's building so he wouldn't have to go home at night if the inspiration was upon him. Edison also demanded similar dedication from his employees, expecting them to work as hard—and as long—as he did. He demanded excellence and he demanded it on a never-ending, constant basis. Work was to be done when Edison deemed it be done, and other people's family or outside obligations were of no concern, even at night and on weekends and holidays, if something "important" was being done at the lab.

Edison's obsession with his work blinded him to the fact that those who worked for and with him might not have the same passion for the process, or the same ability to work without sleep or food. He did not empathize; he did not put himself in his employees' shoes. He demanded, and when his demands were not met, he did not respond charmingly.

Nonetheless, the quality of the work that was produced at the Menlo Park, New Jersey, plant (and the later one in West Orange, which is now a National Historic Site and a museum) where Edison set up shop is indisputable—it can honestly be stated that many of the most influential devices of the twentieth century were developed at the Edison lab, and they were, no doubt, products of Edison's obsessed, tunnel-vision nature. He wasn't charming, but he did create some of the most useful tools ever offered to humankind. It's a trade-off that most of society (minus, perhaps, the workers at Edison's plant) would gladly make.

The point is, Edison managed to rise to the very top of his industry—and, in fact, created a number of industries for him to be at the top of—by having an indisputable, tremendous talent and a thorough knowledge of his business. No one could possibly accuse Thomas Edison of having risen to the top through false or unscrupulous means: he delivered what he promised, and much more. But, charm was not high on his priority list.

Edison was one of the *exceptions that prove the rule.* He did not Charm His Way to the Top; rather, he worked his way to the top by almost consciously eschewing charm entirely and surviving on pure talent and grit. He proves that it's possible to make it to the top without taking the extra steps to be charming, but he also illustrates just how brilliant one must be to accomplish so much without charm as a tool.

Exceptions, actually, don't prove the rule so much as they *underline* it. These people, who manage to get to the pinnacle of their professions without courtesy or charm, don't disprove the utility of charm itself—in fact, they emphasize it. Because we see through their example just how difficult it is to succeed without charm, we can draw from their experience the knowledge that with charm, the same things can be accomplished. But the process will be somewhat easier, and considerably more enjoyable.

There's also the problem of the fall after the rise. While Edison never had to contend with a fall from grace (he died a legend in his own time), his case was not malicious or actively rude—he simply didn't have the time or the patience to be charming, and didn't see the need for it. Others, who have fewer and dimmer gifts than Edison, have reached the acme of their professions, only to drop from those heights when either the industry in which they worked changed, or when they made too many mistakes.

Without charm to help, these people find it difficult to rebound. The coworkers and competitors they abused during their rise and their stay at the top are not disposed toward helping; in fact, most will be happy to turn their backs on someone who exhibited nothing but narcissism and contempt for others. Lack of charm here is not just the absence of a helpful tool, but really a deadly weapon being used against the person no longer at the top.

It's not as if these people were unable to learn the same principles of charm we're discussing in this book—they just didn't bother to do so, based either on arrogance or an inability to recognize the problem. They *could* have learned the value of a smile, a kind word, a thank-you note, or a sympathetic ear, but they chose to focus instead on their own accomplishments and the next strategic step, rather than the people such steps affect. The exceptions that prove the rule also prove another: the bigger they are, the harder they fall.

Given that knowledge, your own quest for increased charm should be fueled a little more fully now. You can't just focus on the climb to the top—those who have achieved fame and wealth will tell you it's a lot harder to *stay* there—and without charm, the ability to maintain success is much more difficult.

Also, the idea of reaching "the top" is somewhat vague—in most businesses, there is no clearly defined "top." There is always something more to accomplish, more that can be done. If you consider the process less of a journey with a distinct destination, and more a quest for something that keeps changing shape and direction, you'll have a better view of what you're trying to accomplish. The person who dies with the most expensive toys doesn't win. It's the one who lives the life he really wants who comes out ahead.

In order to accomplish *that*, it's important to think about others, because other people are on this planet for us to meet and explore— they are part of the journey, and we are part of theirs. If we can bring someone along the way, the dark passages probably won't be as scary, and the ultimate destination will be much more pleasant.

A key element of charm, you'll recall, is convincing people you care about them. This will be considerably more effective, and easier to do, if it is also true. And it will make your trip to the top more satisfying if you can point to the people you met along the way, some of whom you managed to bring with you, and know they are just as glad to have met you as you are to have met them.

Charm is a personality trait, a commodity, a tool, a weapon, and a talent. Used effectively and skillfully, it can help you accomplish many of the things you hope to do in life. Without it, you might accomplish just as much, but you will have to work that much harder to do so, and the process might be that much less enjoyable.

Why would anyone *choose* to be the exception that proves the rule, when they could do just as much and have charm, as well?

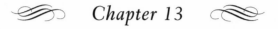 *Chapter 13*

Being Charmed

Those who have learned, practiced, and cultivated their own inner charm live with a knowledge that they have a tool, an opportunity, to use it whenever they deem it necessary. This is an extraordinary feeling, and one that you'll truly cherish.

But with that knowledge comes its flip side—the assurance that others possess at least some of the same talents, and therefore might be using it on us as we go through our daily lives. Under most circumstances, this is a very pleasant experience, as being charmed is at least as enjoyable as charming someone else. But under some circumstances, particularly business scenarios, the possibility that charm might hide some other motive must be raised, and that can become something of a problem.

Does being charmed mean being taken? Not necessarily, but it is an unfortunate sign of our times that we even have to ask the question, or consider the possibility. Sometimes, people really *are* trying to take advantage of you, and a smiling face coupled with a smooth and friendly approach can mask intentions that are not the ones the words being said profess.

So, given what you know about charm and how it is practiced, how can you determine when the person with whom you're dealing is being sincere and when he or she is being unscrupulous? There is no 100 percent guaranteed formula that will always work, but you can use your own skills, the ones you've developed through observation, practice, and instinct, to give yourself a certain edge. Again, the key here is empathy, but it's not as benign and selfless a process at it was before. Now, you're trying to determine what the other person *wants*, and how he or she is planning to get it.

First, it's important to know how to determine exactly whether someone is sincere or not in the charming things they do or say. That's never easy, but it's often possible, and the skills you need are the same ones you use in cultivating your own personal charm. That's the good news.

Begin by evaluating the situation. In a job interview, obviously the potential employee's goal is to come across as competent and charming. The employer doing the interview is more apt to be businesslike and pay less attention to charm (that's a gross generalization, but it's a way to help evaluate the goals for both parties). In other words, the employee is trying to *get* something, and the employer is trying to find the right person to whom it should be given.

Remember, in every relationship (business, personal, or any type in between), there is a *seller* and a *buyer*. The seller's job is to make something seem more attractive and interest the other party in acquiring it. The buyer's job is to find the right product and acquire it for a fair price.

In the job interview situation we described above, the interviewer is the buyer. He is interested in finding someone to work for his company, and wants to find the best possible person at a salary the company considers fair and affordable. The person being interviewed is the seller—she is presenting a product (herself) to fill a need the seller wants to satisfy. Her job here is to seem as attractive a product (a potential employee) as possible—competent, eager, industrious—*charming*.

In most situations, there will be a heavier burden on the *seller* to seem charming. The buyer may also benefit from exhibiting charm, and should do so whenever possible, but it is not as crucial a trait for him as it would be for the seller. After all, if the buyer isn't charming, will the seller refuse to sell a product to him? Maybe, but probably not.

Therefore, it's helpful when evaluating any situation to determine who is the seller and who is the buyer. If you are the buyer—either in a literal, retail sense or as someone who can take or leave the situation being discussed—you should still strive to be charming (after all, you might be the seller next time). But you should also notice that the other person has something he wants *you* to buy, and so they may be a little more inclined to "turn on the charm," which often means to fake it, rather than to truly exercise sincere charm.

Charm, from Both Sides, Now

Amelia Kinkade is an author and pet communicator in the Los Angeles area. She's also among the country's top one hundred psychics, and communicates psychically with animals. As it happens, she also happens to be one of the most charming people I've ever met.

Kinkade had written her first book, *Straight from the Horse's Mouth: How to Talk to Animals and Get Answers*, in 2001, and hoped to find someone notable to write the foreword. She attended a

A "gentle" accessible charm is what makes up the Tom Hanks brand. (Rich Schmitt Photography)

Slick or not, few public figures have been considered as universally charming as President Bill Clinton. Even political enemies have been caught saying, "Damn, I like that guy." (Rich Schmitt Photography 🔔·

No one has taught me more about the powers of charm in politics than famous presidential advisor Dick Morris. (Collection of the author) 🔔

Known as the "cute" Beatle, Paul McCartney has been charming audiences both personally and musically for more than four decades. (Rich Schmitt Photography 🖼️)

Paramount head Sherry Lansing can say "no" to a deal in such a charming way that she makes you feel like she just said "yes." (Rich Schmitt Photography) 🐌

After eight years of Clinton's charisma, the nation found President George W. Bush's "everyman" likeability refreshing. (Rich Schmitt Photography) 🐌

What you see is what you get with Billy Crystal. He's just as comfortable hosting the Academy Awards with an audience of a billion people as he is at a baseball game. (Rich Schmitt Photography) 🐌

Both personally and publicly, Arnold Schwarzenegger's infectious enthusiasm "pumps" people up. (Rich Schmitt Photography)

Sandra Bullock has epitomized the words "cute" and "charming" throughout her career. (Rich Schmitt Photography)

By being a bit humble, at least by Hollywood's standards, Jennifer Aniston has charmed her way into America's heart. (Rich Schmitt Photography)

Although unquestionably a musical genius, Michael Jackson should refrain from opening up a charm school, at least currently. (Rich Schmitt Photography) 🐿🌰

convention in San Francisco and heard Dr. Bernie S. Siegel, one of the country's most noted oncologists and a best-selling author, deliver the keynote address.

"I had decided by the end of the speech that the one person I *wasn't* going to ask about the foreword was Bernie Siegel," she recalls. Noting that everyone at the well-attended conference seemed to want something from Dr. Siegel, she opted instead to offer him something if they met.

They did meet, a few minutes after the speech was over, in an elevator. Kinkade introduced herself and told Dr. Siegel a little about what she does. But then she did something very smart. She offered *him* help, in any way, if he ever needed such a thing. She gave Dr. Siegel a brochure and business card, and said never to hesitate if there was anything she could do for him.

Kinkade began the day as the *seller* in the relationship. She needed someone to write a foreword for her book, and wanted a prominent person like Dr. Siegel to do so. But she realized that Dr. Siegel has people trying to sell him things all day long, every day, and felt the best approach was to avoid selling.

Dr. Siegel remembered her, and three days later, when Kinkade arrived home again, he called. It seemed he had been watching his son Steven's cat while the young man was away, and the cat had vanished, lost in very dangerous coyote territory. Dr. Siegel, distraught over the problem, said he was skeptical of the claims Kinkade made about being able to communicate psychically with animals, but he was desperate. Would she help?

Of course she would. The first thing Kinkade heard was the name "Michael," and she told Dr. Siegel, "The cat wants Michael." Michael, he informed her, was the name of the veterinarian his son brought the cat to see. "That means the cat is alive," Kinkade told him.

Late that night, Kinkade sent Dr. Siegel an e-mail detailing the area where she believed the cat to be. And the next morning, she received a reply labeled "SUCCESS!" that informed her the cat was found in precisely the spot she had diagrammed.

Dr. Siegel had now become the buyer, asking for something from Kinkade and receiving a service. She never had to ask him to write the foreword for her book—he insisted on it, after having written more than one article on the experience and mentioning her to a crowd during a speaking engagement.

"Bernie would be insulted if I didn't ask him for something now," she says today. Among other things, Dr. Siegel has helped Kinkade with introductions to producers at the *Today* show and editors at large city newspapers. She has never asked him for any assistance, but because she helped when she could, Dr. Siegel volunteers. Where Kinkade might have tried to be a seller, asking Dr. Siegel for his help, she does not have that responsibility now. Why? Because she was charming.

Dr. Siegel, in the example above, had numerous reasons to question Amelia Kinkade's charm. Here was a woman he'd never met, whom he was clearly in a position to help if he chose to, and she never asked for anything. Instead, she offered her assistance should it be needed. She made claims many people would find difficult to believe, but did not request anything from him, not even a fee for her services. She merely told him she admired his speech, that she had come to the conference to meet him (which wasn't a lie, but was an exaggeration—she had come to meet many of the people there, and he was easily the most prominent), and then offered to help him or his family with her own special talent, if needed.

Surely Dr. Siegel had met a good number of people at the conference Kinkade attended, and probably many of them wanted something of him—an endorsement, help with an ill family member, a publishing contact—but how many of them chose to offer *him* something? Just one. The one who got what she needed.

Did Kinkade have an agenda when she arrived at the conference? Certainly she did. "The meek will *not* inherit the earth," she is fond of saying, and to prove it, she had traveled to San Francisco to find someone to write a foreword for her book. But once the keynote address was completed, and Kinkade saw the many people swarming around Dr. Siegel, she decided he would probably see her as just another seller, and her chances were slim.

But once the opportunity presented itself, her approach was unexpected and extraordinary. It was also sincere—she really was willing to help him or his family when necessary, and it was necessary very soon afterward. Kinkade never hesitated, and she never tried actively to benefit from the request Dr. Siegel made. His gratitude and his own reaction to her charm made it unnecessary for Kinkade ever to ask him for assistance.

Alas, not every encounter will be as pure and sincere as the one described above. Some people really *will* use charm to get whatever they want, and there will be occasions when what they want will be in conflict with what you want or need to succeed in business. So consider the roles being played. Are you the buyer or the seller?

If you are the seller, trying to get someone to believe in your product or your business (or yourself), the responsibility to be charming is mostly yours. You will usually be more aware of the other person's needs—since you are bidding to fill them—and therefore you will do your best to empathize and anticipate problems the buyer might have. You will go out of your way to accommodate and to make a favorable impression.

If your role in the relationship is that of the buyer, however, you should—as the adage warns—beware. The other person probably has more to gain, and more to lose, in the transaction, and knows that. The smile you see on his face might be sincere, but it might not. The compliments you're being paid might be meant just to flatter, and not to truly appreciate your hard work. The offers of assistance and loyalty you hear might very well be as heartfelt and string-free as Kinkade's—but they might not.

Your ability to step into the other person's shoes should serve you well in both roles. Obviously, as the seller, your well-cultivated talent for empathy will help determine what the buyer needs and which aspects of your message are most likely to provide it. As the buyer, being able to see through another's eyes can help you in an attempt to determine motive and—most important—the next step in the process. Anticipation, particularly in a negotiating situation, can be especially crucial, and being able to determine what the other person is thinking (without the help of a psychic like Kinkade) is undeniably useful in protecting yourself and furthering your agenda.

It's not the ability to see into another's thoughts that is being used here. It is the ability to determine what *you* would do in that situation, given the other person's needs and wants. You can't think for someone else, but you can discern what that person is trying to gain, and determine whether or not it is helpful to you for the other person to achieve that goal.

In the case of Kinkade and Dr. Siegel, mutual goals were accomplished, and that should always be the optimum goal. Dr. Siegel not only got back his son's pet, he also discovered a topic for discussion at his many speaking engagements, and for at least two articles. He also made a friend and an ally, and that is invaluable.

Amelia Kinkade benefited greatly from her encounter with Dr. Siegel, and she did it by making the most of her very considerable charm. She thought about what it must be like to be Dr. Bernie S. Siegel, and guessed correctly. She offered, then, something that he probably doesn't hear very often, and when called upon, delivered something he probably could not have gotten from anyone else. She received the publicity boost for her book that she had sought, as well as an extremely prestigious foreword for her book and a devoted friend. Charm has served Kinkade very, very well.

The same can work for you. Now, keep in mind that Kinkade was determined at that conference to complete her mission, and once she is on a trail, it is remarkably difficult to get her to stray from it. Her message about the meek is not unimportant—sometimes, it takes nerve to be charming.

It also takes nerve to be underhanded and sneaky, and you have to be able to recognize such traits when you see them. Most people walk through life asking themselves mentally: "What's in it for *me?*" Those who use charm successfully in business and personal matters walk through life with a different question on their minds: "What's in it for *them?*" By answering that question, they manage to answer the first for themselves without any effort.

Charm is not simple, and it is not easy. But when it is understood properly, it can be a very powerful thing.

After all, Dr. Siegel's son still has that cat.

Chapter 14

Turnabout: Fair Play?

So far, we have assumed that you are as pure in your plans and tactics as Amelia Kinkade was in her dealings with Dr. Bernie Siegel. And you probably are. But let's face it, there are some people you just don't like, and you have to work with (or for) some of them. It's not always so easy to be charming when in the presence of someone you actively dislike.

Here, then, is an important question: If someone you don't like, perhaps a rival within your company or a competitor, asks you for help, will you provide it, given the charming demeanor you have worked so hard to cultivate? And consider the reverse. If you need help, can you go to someone who works hard at maintaining charm, but might not necessarily be a friend, or even an ally?

Very few among us are saints. Our natural impulse when dealing with those we see as threats, or those we just plain don't like, is not to be kind and helpful and . . . charming. We are probably more likely to turn our backs on such people when they are having difficulty, and perhaps even to quietly revel in their discomfort. That doesn't make us bad people. It's not a ringing recommendation for us as a species, but we humans tend to react with emotion, rather than thought, when given the choice.

Is there another side to this story? Does it *really* make sense to turn the other cheek and lend a hand when we know the beneficiary of our good deed would probably stab us in the back if given the chance? Maybe part of being charming is to try to be just a little bit better than we might normally be—maybe that is the way that we project our charm to others in some circumstances.

No business will succeed by helping its competition, but by choosing to use charm and compassion in dealing even with those who are in opposition to our goals, we can set an example and create a reputation that will enhance and forward our business.

That doesn't mean you have to do something detrimental to your own interests in order to cultivate your reputation. It doesn't mean you have to shoot yourself in the foot, or cut off your nose to spite your face, or any other idiom you think fits this example. You are not obligated to hurt yourself in the name of charm. But by not giving in to impulses that may seem natural—for example, the pleasure we might take at seeing a competitor in jeopardy—we can make ourselves look good to the outside world while continuing to do everything we need to keep our business healthy and prosperous.

At the same time, we must keep vigilant. Those charmers with whom we're doing business may not have our best interest at heart, as we saw in the previous chapter. So we have to use our best skills to determine how much we need to do, while watching the competition (be it within our own company or from the outside) for signs of deception.

Remember, too, that it is not necessary to do whatever your colleague or competition wants you to do in order to be charming. Charm does not assume acquiescence or stupidity—you are not required to give in on every point just because you want to be seen as charming.

In today's coarse, crude society, the use of charm is so rare as to be startling, but *false* charm, which reeks of insincerity and snake oil, is rampant. While most people don't bother even to attempt the fake stuff, real charm is still easily distinguishable from the phony substitute, and will be recognized as such.

The problem is that, in many cases, even at some of the highest levels, no attempt is being made at all. In late November 2003, the *New York Times* ran an article depicting the almost total deterioration of any attempt at civility—in the United States Congress.

The article quoted John Podesta, former President Clinton's chief of staff, as saying that there had always been animosity between the two major political parties in the country, but "what is distinct about this period is the failure to really listen to the other side. There is no attempt to work in the center and find a kind of bipartisan middle."

That's what's missing from much of the discourse in business and in personal life today, the ability to give in *a little*, to find common ground. People seem less willing to give up even a bit of what they want in order to accommodate another's needs. And if Congress can't get along, knowing that the country's fate may very well hang in the balance, can we be expected to artfully compromise, even on the smallest of points?

The *Times* quotes Burdett Loomis, a political scientist at the University of Kansas, as noting that in the current climate, "you get the sense that it's deal-making for partisan advantage, rather than trying to come to some approximation of good policy." This, he said, was true of both parties.

Notice that the problem seems to be one of *attitude*, not political point of view. It is an unwillingness to even *consider* the other side's perspective that leads to stalemate, and eventually, to defeat for both sides. Neither Democrats nor Republicans benefit when *nothing* gets done, and still, the personalities involved, given the current climate of rudeness and inconsideration, refuse to see the Big Picture, and concentrate merely on defeating the other side's plans.

This is a perfect recipe for inaction. Keep in mind, even when dealing with those who might oppose you in some way, that if nothing is accomplished, you will not look better to anyone, and your goals, either long- or short term, will not be fulfilled. Is it better to compromise, give up a little of what you hope to achieve and be seen as the peacemaker, or to dig in your heels, refuse to give an inch, and be seen as the obstacle?

It doesn't help when the other party is seen strictly in terms of his opposition to your goal. There is much talk in politics of "the loyal opposition," but legislation is done when partisan affiliations are considered less important than the good of the country. When there is a true necessity—an emergency situation or a looming threat—suddenly, bills are written and passed in no time flat. Why? Because the overall goal for both sides is seen as the same, and the details of which side got which rider added or gave in on some small provision are put on the back burner.

When you are negotiating a contract or holding a meeting to get more business for your company or having a job interview, your goal is clear. The goal of the person (or people) with whom you are dealing might not be as obvious. Particularly when the other parties are not allies of yours, you may feel that what is being said can't necessarily be trusted. This is understandable, but you have to be careful not to let your distrust color the business at hand. Yes, this person might not have your best interests in mind, but if he goes home without having achieved anything, that will not be a help to his interest, either. So you must focus on the common goal, and proceed from there.

If there is a provision in the discussion that is irksome to you, but will not *significantly* affect the outcome of the negotiations, perhaps you should consider giving in on that point. Negotiation is all about compromise, and if you give in on one point, you might expect to be given a concession in return on another point. You shouldn't *insist* upon that sort of give-and-take unless the concession you receive is extremely important, but it is not rude to remind the other party that you did, indeed, compromise on something that he asked for, and would appreciate that kind of consideration in return.

Charm does not require you to be friends with every person who crosses your path—it does require that you treat each person with respect, courtesy, and empathy. That last part is the key. *Empathy* requires listening, and in any kind of business arrangement, listening to the other side's arguments and concerns will not only increase your reputation as a charming colleague, it will also provide you with information beyond what a casual participant would be able to gather.

For example, when negotiating an agreement with another company to use its materials to make your product, you may notice that the representative of the other company twice mentions his product's reliability, despite your having made no inquiries about it. This could be an indicator that you should further research the component's performance before signing a deal. While a casual listener might think only that the other company is proud of its accomplishments, an astute listener who has trained himself to be charming might avoid a serious problem for his company.

This is one example in which the other party's interest is clearly in opposition to your own—if their component is less than reliable, and you don't know that ahead of time, your company might find itself in a very bad situation. This is not the kind of situation in which compromise or accommodation will make you seem more charming; it will only make you seem gullible. You have to stand your ground when there is no upside for your interest, but that is only possible when you have the information you need ahead of time.

Your training in charm will serve you well in areas other than simply making a good impression and being well liked. It will help you develop a second nature, and the intensity of your listening is key to this talent.

Remember, listening isn't simply a question of *hearing* the words the other person is saying. It is also the ability to see the argument *from the other person's viewpoint*, thereby understanding both the words and the motives behind them.

In the course of two decades of working with the biggest names in show business, I have had to develop my ability to see things from the other's point of view. Some people in entertainment are not (as we have seen in previous chapters) the most charming in private. And I have seen behavior that would not be considered charming by any yardstick in any industry. There are a few clients I have asked, for various reasons, to take their business elsewhere, although that has happened very rarely and not always because of the client's behavior.

In short, I have learned to deal with people on a business level whom I would not seek out as friends on a personal level. That is the nature of business generally, and everyone does it in one fashion or another.

Still, I try as hard as I can to be charming, even when dealing with people who are trying as hard as they can *not* to be charming. There are a few reasons for this: first, I consider it everyone's duty to try and raise the level of courtesy and charm for our society—things have reached such a low level that only with effort from as many people as possible will society ever see an improvement.

Also, I have to keep my business in mind at all times. Even if the client with whom I'm dealing (or someone I have to deal with in my service of that client) is being a complete boor, I try to retain my composure and be seen as the peacemaker, the reasonable negotiator, the calming influence. Remember, very rarely is completely idiotic behavior of this sort exhibited in complete privacy—most of the time in the entertainment business, there are groups of people on the site who are involved in the production in one way or another (even at business meetings). So I'm projecting my image of charm to be seen *even if the person being unreasonable isn't the intended audience.* I may very well want to do business with some of the *other* people in the room at some time in the future, and I want them to remember exactly how I handled this situation. I want them to remember it well.

If I conduct myself with considerably more charm than the person who is "acting up," if I manage to make an impression as a calming influence to everyone in the room *except* the person who is being anything but charming, I am doing myself and my business noticeable good. I may not want to be in this situation; I may be ruing the day I ever got involved with this person, but I am going to make sure that when the other people in the room leave that building, they will remember that I was calm, reasonable, and if possible, charming.

That is the best revenge against someone who is acting in a way that could do you harm—to rise above the lack of consideration and be seen as the better person for not having gotten involved in the insanity.

If discretion is the better part of valor, sometimes serenity is the better of charm. *Not* reacting to an intense situation can be as charming as taking quick action under other circumstances. You don't have to deny your feelings when you are badly treated, but it can be more effective to react with calm and level-headed thinking than to charge into battle with an opponent whose true motivations you might never know.

Charm, after all, is about letting the other person know you care, and even if the other person is acting in ways that can be detrimental to you, it isn't a bad idea to care. You don't have to agree. Showing those around the situation (the others in the room) that you care about *their* feelings by doing your best to avoid an embarrassing scene is even more valuable.

Living well, someone once said, is the best revenge. But when you're dealing with a coarse, crude adversary, sometimes charming well is even better.

Chapter 15

All Charm, All the Time

As we have seen, it is not a simple task to plant and nurture the seeds of your own charm to use in business situations. But if you have been reading carefully, you know that charm is not something that should be practiced only during business hours. You need to be aware of your behavior, and the image you project, twenty-four hours a day, seven days a week.

If that sounds daunting, consider the reasons for 24/7 charm:

- Charm is a personality trait, but it is also a practice, and should be treated like any practice—the more you use it, the more proficient you will be.
- Charm is like a muscle—it gets stronger with each exercise. Use it, or lose it.
- You don't know who is going to be the next Bill Gates. If you're disrespectful to the waitress at the diner today, you

might be slighting the CEO whose company is interested in buying yours tomorrow. Maybe she won't remember you, but suppose she did—and it was a *pleasant* memory . . .

- Look at the bigger picture. There isn't enough charm in this world, by far.
- Contribute all you can, and you will truly be doing the human race a great service.

Okay, so maybe that last reason is a little nebulous, but it's not insincere. I really *do* believe that our society needs to respect kindness, courtesy, and charm much more fervently than it does now. We have become as rude and coarse a race of humans as has ever existed since the beginning of civilization. Maybe taking the time to learn the dry cleaner's name isn't important in the grand scheme of things, but does it really hurt you? And doesn't it make you feel better when people take the time to learn *your* name?

Think about this: every day, as you walk down any street, you pass dozens (perhaps hundreds, or thousands, depending on where you live) of people. How many of them actually register in your brain? Not that many—they might as well be the extra soldiers painted into a war movie's panorama by a computer—they are merely obstacles in the way between where you are and where you are going.

Now, think about how easy it would be to make a connection— even a tiny one—with each of those people. In his book *How to Connect in Business in 90 Seconds or Less*, Nicholas Boothman suggests taking note of the color of every person's eyes as they pass. You don't have to *remember* each color, just notice it. That can make an enormous difference in the way you perceive other people and how you are perceived by them.

Why? Because in training yourself to notice the eye color of everyone who passes (or everyone in the meeting, or everyone in the elevator, etc.) you force yourself to look into their eyes, even if just for a fraction of a second. That is the first step toward making a connection with another person and establishing a rapport, which can lead to stronger connections. Now, I don't believe that every person you look in the eye will become a good friend, or even a passing acquaintance (and neither does Boothman), but if it becomes a *habit*, an unconscious thing that you practice over and over so much you can't *not* do it, perhaps you will establish an alliance or two that will make a significant difference in your career or your company's future.

That's worth making the effort, isn't it?

It is that kind of training that can make the difference between what we're defining as charm and what passes for acceptable behavior in today's society. It has come to the point that when someone does go out of his way to make eye contact, we might wonder what his motives are, and feel slightly unnerved by the attention. That's why making sure that the look is accompanied by a sincere, friendly *smile* is equally important.

Boothman suggests standing at a mirror and saying the word "great" over and over. He says to "put your face about ten inches in front of a mirror. Look yourself right in the eye and say the word 'great' in as many different ways as you can: angry, loud, soft, sexy, like Jerry Lewis. . . . Keep going. Eventually you'll crack up. Repeat the exercise once a day for three days. The next time you're going to meet someone, say 'great' under your breath three times, and you'll be smiling."*

I don't know if this technique will work for you, but it's also useful to think of something especially pleasant (a childhood memory, a food you really like, a person you are particularly fond of) just before meeting someone new. It might help your smile to be more natural.

Some men and women I know in business have actually rehearsed their handshake, to best gauge how firm it should be, and how warm.

* Nicholas Boothman, *How to Connect in Business in 90 Seconds or Less* (New York: Workman Publishing, 2002).

This might be going a bit far, but if you feel the need to do so, that is exactly what you should do. The shier and more nervous among us often practice every aspect of a meeting in advance, and therefore feel more comfortable when they sit down for the real meeting. That often makes the person being met feel more at ease, and anything that can accomplish this should be taken seriously, and practiced with great care. Relaxation in dealing with others is perhaps the most important tool of charming your way to the top.

Let's examine this: if you are at ease in your own mind, you are considerably more likely to be thinking clearly, focused on your goals and your techniques, free to react to situations without worry or anxiety, and capable of making intelligent, considered choices. There is no downside—assuming you're not so relaxed that you actually fall asleep in the middle of a presentation.

Now, think about what someone who is on edge might be like in a business or personal meeting (a date, for example). Forgetting to smile, or smiling too broadly to be seen as sincere, this person might be thinking about how he or she looks, rather than what is being said. Important statements could be misunderstood, or missed entirely. The perception would be of someone who is distracted, uninterested, or just plain rude.

Okay, so the first scenario is more attractive than the second, don't we agree?

The trick is in understanding how to be relaxed at the moment when it is most important. Business meetings can indeed be stressful, as anyone in any business knows firsthand. If a job interview for a position you really want, a presentation for a client you truly need, or a meeting with colleagues you honestly respect means enough that it can change your (professional) life, isn't it natural to be nervous?

Of course it is. The thing to remember is that perception in these cases is a large percentage of what will become the truth when the story is told and retold. In other words, the others in your meeting will take away their impressions of your demeanor, and if you *appear* to have been calm, relaxed, and at ease with yourself, it doesn't matter if you were or weren't. What matters is that your preparation made it possible to project that image. In the minds of the people you were trying to impress, you were successful.

The best way to convey that message, to project the image you want to project, is to actually mean it. If you really are calm, you will appear calm, and no matter what the prospective consequences of the meeting, it is possible to enter the room feeling at ease and confident.

10 Ways to Calm Down
(Before a Business Meeting)

1. **Prepare, prepare, prepare.** Confidence is a by-product of preparation. If you know that you have the agenda covered in every possible way, you'll feel sure of yourself ahead of time.

2. **Know your enemy—or your friend.** If you have a strong grasp of the other person's (or people's) point of view, you'll have a much better idea of what to expect, and you can be ready.

3. **Get a grip.** Yes, this meeting, presentation, or conference may seem so vitally important that its success or failure appears to hold your destiny in its hand. But keep your perspective—this is one meeting. If it doesn't go well, you will probably not die. Keep an eye on the big picture, and your anxiety won't be as all encompassing.

4. **Distract yourself.** If you're sufficiently prepared, take your mind away from the meeting until just before it begins. Work on another project, or stay away from work entirely—play computer solitaire. Thinking about something else will keep you calmer.

5. **Don't drink coffee.** Caffeine is not the place to go right now. If anything, go for decaf or stick with water. It seems simple, but many people will overlook this detail, and think a nice, hot beverage will calm them down. It won't.

6. **Take a nap.** You read that right. If you can take the time, and there's a convenient place to do so, try to rest for a while before the meeting. It certainly won't hurt, and it will fulfill a number of the functions of relaxation, like taking your mind off the impending meeting, and giving you enough rest. Besides, it feels decadent and forbidden, even though it's exactly what you need at the moment. Don't let your boss catch you, though, or explain to him or her ahead of time that this is not a habit, but a way to better prepare for a crucial business meeting.

7. **See the other people as they really are.** They used to say that if you wanted to relax when speaking in public to visualize your audience in their underwear. I have never seen the utility in this advice, but I do think it's important to understand that you're not up against a race of Titans who can overcome any obstacle. The people you're about to talk to are in business, like you, and are probably just as nervous as you are. Don't overestimate them.

8. **Don't underestimate them, either.** Preparation, as we said before, is key. But in doing your prep work, make sure you don't become so confident that you fail to take your competition or rivals seriously. Yes, you are well prepared, but so are they. Confidence should come to you because you know what you're doing, not because you think you're better than they are.

9. **Imagine the best—and worst—case scenarios.** If only because you want to know that the End of the World isn't coming,

realistically visualize what will happen if the meeting doesn't go especially well (probably, the consequences will not be as dire as you might have thought). Also, consider what will happen if everything goes well. At the very least, that should be enough to relax you on the way into the conference room.

10. **Remember—you're charming.** You've done a good deal of work practicing and developing your skills, so you should trust them. There's no reason to think that you won't do exactly the right thing given almost any situation. Relax, and charm them!

Even outside the stress of an organized event such as a meeting or conference, you will be cultivating and practicing your charm. Keep it strong as you travel through your day, dealing with everyone who crosses your path.

Wal-Mart is one of the largest businesses in the world, and certainly in the retail industry. Each year, the company seems to open more stores, add more merchandise, and pad the profit sheet with a few more billions. But it is a business that has never forgotten, particularly in the face it shows the public, to display its charm.

In the traditional business plan, for example, there is no provision for a "greeter," who stands at the front of the store, handling questions, giving out balloons or lollipops to children (with parents' permission, of course), and just, well, *greeting* those who enter for a shopping trip. Many corporate executives would consider such an idea a waste of employee time and salary, and would laugh it out of the conference room on its first suggestion.

But the world's largest retailer deems the idea of the greeter not only worth consideration, but important to the plan for each of its stores. Why? Because Wal-Mart knows that its merchandise and its pricing are competitive but not necessarily blatantly superior to its competition. It knows that in order to stand out as a company and a brand, it has to provide something else, something that touches the consumer on an emotional level and makes the store memorable in a positive, friendly way.

In other words, Wal-Mart knows that it's important to be charming. So the greeter, often a local senior citizen (so the company can better show its commitment to the community and its most respected members), is not only a nice idea, but a vital one for the chain.

Notice, also, that the greeter isn't there only when the Christmas buying season rolls around, or on days when the company believes traffic in the stores will be especially high; it's not even just a weekend position. Greeters are in every Wal-Mart store every minute that store is open, because the company is aware that every customer who walks through their doors is important, and should be the beneficiary of the company's charm on a consistent basis.

Think of that when you're going through an average day, seeing the counter help at the Starbucks on the way to work in the morning, saying hello to the waitress at lunch, or introducing yourself to the conductor on the train ride home. There is never a time when it doesn't help to be charming, and there is never a time when it helps *not* to be.

Charm is a 24/7 proposition, and the best part of that is that you'll find it coming more naturally the more you practice. Pay attention to what you're doing, and eventually, charm will be your nature—*not* your second nature, because even that is something you have to consider.

And who knows. Maybe one of the people you encounter in the course of your day will be the next Bill Gates. Or the current Bill Gates. And he will remember you in a positive way.

There's not a thing wrong with *that*.

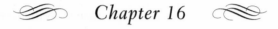

Chapter 16

I Just Don't
Feel Charming Today

As I said earlier in the book, charm does not come as naturally to me as it may to some others. I have had to work at and develop the charm I had instinctively, and to constantly make it a priority to do so. I have consciously cultivated and nurtured the qualities I've observed in those whom I consider charming, have asked them questions about their charm, and learned from them. I have decided to take what I considered to be an area of my personality that was not strong enough, and turn it into one of my greater assets.

That does not mean I feel charming every minute of every day. Even Cary Grant wasn't Cary Grant all the time—sometimes Archie Leach would sneak out and take over. And the same thing will undoubtedly happen to you every once in a while, even after you've cultivated your charm to a level you might not have initially thought possible.

Face it: you're not going to feel charming every day.

Sometimes, after all, it just feels like life and fate are conspiring against you. Maybe your boyfriend dumped you last night; maybe your boss is making noises about downsizing. Could be that your competition is debuting a new product that is rumored to make yours look antiquated. Maybe it's something as trivial as a spot on your tie or your favorite TV show being cancelled. It doesn't matter—you're in a bad mood, and you're determined to let the world know it.

Bad move.

Charm isn't something you can reserve for the days when you're feeling chipper. It's a tool you need *all* the time, in every situation you face every day of your life. If you fail to use your charm because you're in a bad mood today, it's entirely possible you'll let down your guard enough to do damage to your efforts and retard your progress.

But that's not the whole downside. Charm, as I've said before, is like a muscle—you use it or lose it. And if you give in to your dark mood today, let it overwhelm the work you've done and the foundation you've laid, you're making it easier for yourself to do the same thing tomorrow, or next Wednesday, or whenever it feels like the gods have once again let you down. That could be disastrous, because it could lead to any number of days when you discard the training you've undergone and the work you've done, and at that point, your charm will become a distant memory, not a tool you can use whenever it suits you.

The only logical plan, then, is to be charming even when—*especially* when—you don't feel like it.

For one thing, you can't plan when you're going to have a bad day or a grouchy mood. These things happen randomly, and are not within our control. So it's important to fight against the inclination to simply surrender to the pressures of the day and act accordingly, because your bad mood or your bad fortune might just pop up on the day of your important business conference with the company that's thinking of buying you out. It might come when your boss is, unbeknownst to you, writing up employee evaluations. It might happen when your competition is about to inaugurate a new ad campaign that makes your company look old and tired.

You can't plan ahead for bumps in the road, but you *can* plan ahead for bumps in your charm. You can avoid them with practice and forethought, and that is exactly what you must do.

It sounds simpler than it is in practice. All you have to do, after all, is harness your emotions and make a logical decision based on the facts you've learned. You know from reading this book what an important asset your charm can be, and you've been given numerous examples of the ways in which it can enhance not only your career, but your life overall. If you weren't convinced, you wouldn't have read this far, so there's no point in my trying to recount the importance of using charm in every possible situation.

Still, it's one thing to know intellectually what should be done, and another to react to a situation that drips with emotion and *not* be caught up in the heat of the moment. Even Mr. Spock wrestled with his emotional side every once in a while on *Star Trek*. It's part of the nature that lives in all of us. Emotion is more powerful than logic, but not necessarily right.

When you're going through that rough patch and the world seems to have it in for you, logic is not necessarily the first thing that will appeal to you. You'll want that emotional outlet, that "steam valve " that vents our emotions and makes us feel purged. And you will have that, but you have to choose the time and the place with . . . logic.

Common sense dictates that the office is not a good place for emotional outbursts, which is why it's so baffling that we've all observed a good number of such scenes in day-to-day work activity. It just seems that people's emotions get the best of them and become so intense as to be uncontrollable, and when that happens, emotions erupt with a violence that is not only distracting, but entirely inappropriate for the business atmosphere. It can also be damaging to one's career.

Yes, the boss often vents at employees as well, and while my own record is not 100 percent clear on the subject, I try my best not to lose my control when dealing with my staff. It's not pleasant, it's not good policy, and the fact is, it usually doesn't help the situation at all. Most of the time, it just heightens tension to have a tantrum—even if it is justified.

Most of the time, in my experience, when a person in a management position loses emotional control and "reams out" an employee, the incident has the opposite effect of what must have been intended. Productivity is *decreased*, rather than increased, as the staff inevitably spends a good deal of time afterward discussing the incident, and not getting work done on time. The manager has *decreased* his authority, rather than having enhanced it, since he is now considered somewhat unstable by the staff, and not entirely rational. Rarely does such an outburst inspire respect and loyalty. Instead, a good number of your best employees may immediately start updating their résumés and looking for a job with someone who can approach things with a calm demeanor.

By the same token, an employee who vents anger, frustration, or simple ambition at a peer or a supervisor is going to be seen as duplicitous, unstable, emotionally fragile, and unreasonable—at best. There isn't any way that losing your cool—and your charm—in the workplace is going to enhance your reputation or your chances for increased success.

Clearly, then, it's best to drop your charm and take out your frustrations on people in your personal life, right? Uh . . . you really haven't been reading very carefully, have you?

It is entirely inappropriate to allow a bad mood or a streak of bad luck, even attached to your career, to spill over into your private life, even if this is exemplified by an encounter as casual as ordering a Big Mac. The person behind the counter isn't the source of your anger, even if it has taken an inordinate amount of time for that burger to be served. If you were in a good mood to begin with, the delay wouldn't bother you in the least—you might even joke about it. But now, because of the upheaval in your emotional life brought on by . . . any-thing . . . you are not behaving like yourself. You are not reacting to minor irritants as the tiny problems they are; you are acting as if your life depended on the speed of the fast-food counter help. And that is *your* problem of proportion, not the person's behind the counter.

Well, then, what area of life is left in which it's okay to release the "steam valve?" It's not healthy or beneficial in any way to keep all your emotion bottled up inside, so there has to be *some* haven, some space in your life where you can let out those feelings you've been having, and deal with them honestly and therapeutically. A few suggestions:

- **Mr. Fist, Meet Mr. Punching Bag.** Physical activity can certainly have a cathartic effect when done properly. Find a type of exercise that suits you, and let it rip as hard as you can. On top of everything else, you will probably end up with a healthier body.
- **Be creative, literally**. If something's bothering you enough to think about it obsessively, it can be turned into a short story, a novel, a painting, a sculpture, a song, a screenplay, a poem, or an opera. Wherever your instinct leads you is the right place. You never have to have your work performed, produced, or published if you don't care to try, but you can certainly work out a lot of messy emotion through the creative process. Write

a murder mystery and kill off the people you don't like. On the page.

ᵉ᷎᷎ **Karaoke night.** When "primal scream" therapy was in vogue, it was argued that letting negative emotions out through a vocal expression of the deepest feelings was therapeutic, and there is sense in that. But if you can do the same singing the blues, rapping to the beat, singing second tenor, or yelling at the umpire for botching the strike call, do that. After a good scream at people who won't be hurt by it, you'll feel better.

ᵉ᷎᷎ **The talking cure.** If stress has become such a problem that you can't control it on your own, there's no shame in seeking out help. Therapists are extremely well practiced at dealing with people who have found bumps in the road, and showing them ways around them. If you need help, get it. It *never* makes sense to ignore a problem.

My longtime friend and client Robert Evans, the legendary film producer (*Chinatown, The Godfather, Love Story*) whose life story has been an autobiographical book and film called *The Kid Stays in the Picture*, is one of the most charming men I've ever met. Mr. Evans understands flattery, he knows sincerity, he knows when to be firm in his position and when to accommodate. He's had a good deal of trouble in his life, and has had to deal with it. Robert Evans knows what it is to have a bad day, and to not want to be charming.

Even when his troubles were at their peak (and they involved drug problems, marital problems, professional problems, and legal problems—all at once), Mr. Evans knew how to use his charm, and how to avoid losing it. He faced up to the consequences of his own wrong actions, fought against charges that he had done more wrong than he actually had, and persevered. It was a long time before he handled a big studio production again, but he got back to where he wanted to be, and is now again an active producer in Hollywood. Currently, he even has an animated television show on the air starring Robert Evans as himself: Comedy Central's *Kid Notorious*.

Without detailing Mr. Evans's life (I refer you to his own book), it is worth noting that he always knew, from his days as a young actor in Hollywood, that charm could help him get where he wanted to go. It wasn't the *only* tool he used, by any stretch of the imagination, and some days, even Mr. Evans will admit, he was not as charming as he hoped to be. Yet, there wasn't a time when he didn't at least know how to be charming if he needed to.

He knows that it's a constant practice, not one that can be "flipped on" like an electrical switch when it's needed. And he uses it to this day.

It would have been just as easy—easier, in fact—for Robert Evans to have fought back against Hollywood when it seemed there wasn't a place for him there. He had a lot of stories to tell, and could have done so, probably to the tune of millions in those days. His public life, married to such beauties as Ali MacGraw, Catherine Oxenberg, and Phyllis George, was the stuff of tabloid sensationalism, and there was a great thirst for the "inside story." Mr. Evans, however, knew that he wanted a future in Hollywood. He chose not to embarrass and expose people he could have ruined, and instead kept using his own charm to work his way back to a position of creativity and control. He has a number of projects in the works in Hollywood as you read this.

The fact is, charm is the art of making it look easy to be charming. We believe in Cary Grant, Tom Hanks, and James Stewart because they don't seem to be *trying* to charm us, but they are doing just that most of the time. They're just exceptionally good at hiding the machinery—you can't see the wheels turning and the gears grinding, so you assume there's no effort involved.

That is what we all aim to do—to be charming and make it look natural. For some lucky individuals, charm *is* natural, but it's always an effort, even for them.

Charm is really a series of decisions, made in sequence, all with a common goal. If we decide that we're going to be charming to this person, every choice we make in the course of this conversation, this encounter, this business meeting, or this relationship will be based on that decision. We react to each situation with the idea, first and foremost, that charm will be our goal. And that will help to point us in the proper direction in our decision making.

If we keep our goal in mind as we proceed, we can get past the occasional obstacle and keep making the proper decisions. We can smile when we need to smile, even if we're grinding our teeth just a bit. We can muster a sincere compliment, even when we wish we could run and hide. And we can continue to charm our way to the top, even when the world seems to be doing its best to discourage us.

It's a choice, not a foregone conclusion.

Chapter 17

Thank-you Notes?
In This Day and Age?

"Etiquette" is an unfortunate, outdated word, but the fact is, the concept it describes does have relevance today, and nowhere does it better apply than in the business world.

The fact is that etiquette, despite its image of lace napkins and Emily Post, is really all about being courteous. It's about doing things in a proper manner so as to make other people feel comfortable and welcome. It's about thinking about someone else's needs (and, by extension, society's needs) ahead of your own in certain situations.

In other words, it's about charm.

Earlier, I made the distinction between charm and courtesy by describing a possible encounter in an elevator. Holding the elevator door for someone is *courtesy*, while complimenting that person on her clothing once inside the elevator is *charm*.

Still, courtesy is worth exploring, particularly in its relationship to etiquette and charm. Each has qualities that lend an advantage to relationships, either personal or business-related. Each concentrates on your dealings with others. Each relies on expectations and fulfillments to make its point. And each, in its own way, can help you succeed in a business context.

Courtesy

When we talk about being "courteous," it's often about things we learned, or should have learned, as children. It's courteous to say "please" or "thank you," to give someone your seat on the bus, to say "bless you" when another person sneezes. Courtesy is more instinctive, yet more practiced and automatic, than either etiquette or charm, and it is the one attribute most often *expected* rather than appreciated in society.

Courtesy is the baseline. It is the minimum that should be expected from all members of society. Unfortunately, we have reached a point in our evolution in which courtesy is so rarely exhibited, we have learned to expect nothing from our fellow humans. It has taken on an air of something extraordinary and unexpected, and become a rarity, a luxury that most people find unusual and amazing. That's a societal shame.

The meat of courtesy consists of common niceties that were once taken for granted: holding open a door, responding promptly to an invitation, showing up to a meeting on time. The phrase "common courtesy" once meant much more than it does today, because courtesy *was* common; the general public practiced it as a rule. Today, a person who opens a door or is meticulous about showing up on time for appointments is considered charming strictly because he lacks competition. If no one else is observing the "common" courtesies, those who do are seen as especially giving and generous individuals.

Just try it. Spend a day noticing and observing the common courtesies. Help someone on with her coat. Let pedestrians pass when you
don't have to. Show up a few minutes *early* for an appointment.

My friend Jeff Cohen, a freelance writer and author of mystery
novels such as *For Whom the Minivan Rolls* and *A Farewell to Legs*,
reports that his daughter recently brought home a test from her sixth
grade class. The paper had been graded and given an A+, with 97
points out of 100 correct. Jeff looked over the paper and noted that the
teacher had actually marked correct two incorrect answers, for a total
of 6 points, and the grade should have been 94 points out of 100.

His daughter said she had noticed that, too, and pointed it out to
the teacher. The teacher, so impressed that a student would tell the
truth about such a matter, allowed the girl to keep her elevated grade
(it wouldn't have made a large difference—an A+ or an A in sixth
grade probably won't determine admission into Harvard) because she
was honest about it.

The point Jeff made was that the teacher *shouldn't* have been
impressed by his daughter's honesty—she should have *expected* it.
But since the standards in today's society are so low, a girl who would
risk a slightly lower grade because it was the right thing to do stands
out in the crowd.

It's the same thing in your business. By performing the common
courtesies, by simply doing what you should be doing as a matter of
course, you can stand out and impress those who might be able to
advance your business or your career. Courtesy, in the form of a few seconds of your time or a handwritten note, is not to be underestimated.

Etiquette

There is a major difference between courtesy and etiquette. Where
courtesy is a reflexive group of "common" activities meant to show

respect for another human being regardless of your relationship with that person, etiquette is another story altogether.

Etiquette does not assume blind adherence to rules without clear definition. It does not require you to size up the situation and decide whether it is to be exercised. Etiquette sets out a specific, codified list of rules for certain situations, and demands that they be followed without question, no matter what.

Various situations will have their separate rules of etiquette. Diplomatic affairs, for example, often have extremely elaborate sets of rules for each detail: who enters first, who bows to whom, who speaks when, and so on. At formal dinner parties, etiquette is followed down to the smallest details, including the seating chart, the setting of each place at the table, the making of toasts, and many others.

Even at less formal occasions, such as business meetings or dates, there is an etiquette to follow. It's not always done anymore, but it is still expected that men will stand when a woman enters the room. At a restaurant, a man will often hold a woman's chair as she sits. In a business meeting, the more senior executive will often sit at the head of the table. Usually, there is an order in which people will talk at such a meeting, and while there is discussion, the order is often followed.

Indeed, *Robert's Rules of Order*, the standard by which government and many business meetings are held, is really an etiquette primer for those who need to know the rules of action in formal meetings. In government, some of the rules are imposed by law, but others are simply kept because they are the accepted rules that have always been followed, and since everyone knows (or should know) what they are, they are agreeable to all. There is a formal etiquette for changing the rules when necessary, as well.

Etiquette expects the rules to be followed without question, and without exception. There is no appeals process, other than to change the rules, and then, only by agreement among the majority of people involved. With etiquette, behavior is not contingent on your evaluation of the other person's feelings or motives; etiquette sets the rules, and they are to be followed in all cases. There is no decision-making process involved.

Charm does not enter into etiquette, except that one makes the commitment to follow the rules set and then does so. It's not easy to stand out from the crowd by employing etiquette, since by definition, etiquette demands that *everyone* follow the same rules. Only by *not* following the rules will you be noticed, and usually not in a positive light.

Charm

Charm is another animal altogether. Charm is going the extra mile, giving the (mathematically impossible) 110 percent, doing more than is expected in any situation—but, it adds another twist. Charm expects that not only are you doing more, you are doing more *with the other person in mind*.

By investing time and effort into developing charm, a person makes a commitment toward a different way of thinking, one that is not required by courtesy or etiquette. Charm means having to consider the other person's point of view *before* your own. It means that you're considering what that person wants from this exchange, and whether or not you'll deliver it. Then, it requires that you determine *how* you will deliver what the person wants (if you make that decision, but in most cases, charm will lean in that direction). Yes, your own interests are important and included in the process, but they are not exclusive and are sometimes secondary.

So what does it mean to have charm and exhibit it in a business atmosphere? It means you have to combine all three elements, courtesy, etiquette, and charm, and use them in creative and memorable new ways.

I am well known among my friends and colleagues as a complete and total nut on the subject of thank-you notes. I insist upon sending them for anything that seems to require acknowledgment: a gift, no matter how small; a meal, even for business purposes; a gesture of any sort that is offered by someone else and improves my reputation or my chances at success. I send more thank-you notes per year than I can tell you about, some of them homemade with photographs I've taken or with a quotation I think is appropriate and memorable. I make sure that the note fits the occasion and the recipient.

Now, I should quickly say that some people think I send too many thank-you notes. They are wrong; the rest of the world doesn't send nearly enough, in my opinion. This is a combination of the three disciplines. It should be common courtesy to thank someone for doing you a favor of any kind—acknowledgment of kindness is basic, and costs nothing (other than a card and a stamp). Etiquette demands a note, as a formal acknowledgment and a tangible record of that acknowledgment (you can *prove* you thanked them, if you have to!). And now that society has deteriorated to the point where no one else sends thank-you notes, yes, you can be seen as an extremely charming person with a very low-cost gesture that may seem antiquated, but is actually as up to date as Madonna's latest identity.

But the thank-you note is just the tip of the iceberg, if you don't mind the mixed metaphor. There are many more gestures that should be routine in daily business but are now considered either passé or unnecessary. Try them and you'll stand out like a shiny polished gold nugget in a stream of dirty rocks.

ƺ Show up *on time* for every meeting. In fact, show up *early*. Arriving late is as rude as you can be, and that's a way of standing out that's really not what you're aiming at.

⤸ Send *gifts*—and I'm not talking about expensive, huge gifts—
to those who do you business favors. Not a pen with your
company's name on it, but it doesn't have to be a Ferrari,
either. The first time I spoke to Amelia Kinkade, she sent me
a calendar with a note specifying the date and time we'd agreed
to meet—very charming, and a great reminder. When I interviewed a woman named Dawn for an internship, she reached
into her bag and produced a bottle of Dawn dishwashing
liquid. It was quite charming—and I remembered her name.

⤸ The smallest gestures are the impressive ones nobody bothers
with anymore—make *eye contact* in conversation; *smile*
sincerely when you meet someone, and *listen, listen, listen.*
Damian Carville, who has held senior sales positions at major
companies such as Sharp Electronics, says most people "confuse listening with waiting for their turn to speak." Actively
listening may be the most charming thing you can do, and no
one can even see you doing it.

Charm is a cumulative process, something that is pieced together from
tiny parts that make up much more than their sum. There will be a
thousand decisions made in your mind today, a high percentage of
them related to your business. If your aim with most of them is tied to
your desire to be charming, you will be charming. It's that simple.

But don't eliminate gestures you feel are no longer relevant, or shy
away from things you think might be seen as outdated, if you believe
they are appropriate and might be seen in a positive light. You should
keep a sense of perspective, certainly—putting down your coat over a
mud puddle like Sir Walter Raleigh is likely to gain you a reputation
that's less charming and more flaky, and besides will result in horrifying dry cleaning bills—but sending a note when you could e-mail is

not an embarrassing anachronism, it's a demonstration of courtesy and charm. With a little etiquette thrown in.

As with all other things that we've discussed, this is part of an effort to rise above the unkind level of discourse to which this world has sunk. Standing out from the crowd can be an asset or a detriment, but when your goal is to be as charming as possible, and you work with that in mind, making every gesture with a charming goal, you will be seen as someone who goes the extra mile.

Without millions of dollars to back us up, many of us have to get by in business with the strength of our determination and our own ideas. Because we've decided that we're going to charm our way to the top, we have committed to thinking a certain way *all the time*. That has taken training, observation, and tons of practice, but it can and will pay off in reputation and business gains. The gestures I've outlined here—and there are countless more—are only a reflection of that mind-set, the way you show other people that you care about them, which is the cornerstone of charm.

A thank-you note? In this day and age? You bet. Think of the last time you received one, especially a handwritten one with a personalized message about the gift you sent, the lunch you bought, the favor you performed. You have to think back quite a way, don't you? That's a shame, but if you do business with me, you probably don't have to think back nearly as far. I will continue with my notes, because I see them as an asset and, more important, I think they are the right thing to do.

It's a tiny gesture, but one that can make a very, very large impression. That's the kind of thing every businessperson should be seeking, every minute of every day.

Chapter 18

Consistency Is All

I make it a point, as I've mentioned, to send a birthday card to many friends and associates. This lets them know I remember them, think warmly of them, and consider their feelings enough to recall the day they were born. It's a very charming gesture, I think.

But if I did it once, and then never again, it would be the polar opposite of charming—it would be approaching the level of an insult. Why? Because it's worse to do something charming once and then never again than it is to never do it at all.

Think about that. *It is worse to do something charming once and then never again than it is to never do it at all.*

If I never sent you a birthday card and we weren't especially close friends or relatives, you probably wouldn't notice. But if I were to send you one this year, you'd probably note how thoughtful and, yes, charming a gesture that would be.

That's fine, but if next year's date rolled around and you received no card, you'd wonder exactly what message I am sending. I cared about you last year, but not this one? I simply forgot, and you weren't sufficiently important that I'd have a reason to remember? That you were useful to me in some way last year, and now you're not? Is that the kind of friend I am?

Consistency is extremely important in charming your way to the top. It's not enough that you are trying to put your best face forward at all times, and it's not enough that you're conscious of it every hour of every day. It's also crucial that you are seen as *consistently* charming, not just an opportunist who chooses to "turn on the charm" when it suits him and ignores it the rest of the time. You can't shift your efforts to be charming from one person to another as one person becomes less capable of helping you and one person becomes more.

The difference between a reputation as a slick, somewhat slimy con artist who uses flattery as a weapon and one as a sincere, salt-of-the-earth friend who would give you the shirt off his back is consistency. For someone who has trained himself to use charm, it's not a terribly difficult trait to exercise—but it is a very important one, and not to be taken lightly.

As with many things associated with charm, consistency is sadly lacking in most areas of life these days. A favorite restaurant might serve a fantastic dish one week, only to have the quality slip when a different chef is cooking on another night. An actor might make one blockbuster hit, then follow it up with a film so bad it's amazing the same star agreed to do both roles. A business associate might think enough of you to recommend your services to his company, but fail to look favorably in your direction when he changes jobs.

Even in smaller details, consistency is faltering—and in places where it was once a solid thing. Go into a McDonald's in a suburban neighborhood and you might still find the clean, fast, friendly atmosphere that was described in all those TV commercials you remember from growing up. Go into another McDonald's outlet in a large city's downtown and the same menu could be offered in a facility where the service is at best indifferent, the atmosphere is downright hostile, and cleanliness is next to impossible.

If a consumer, an employer, or a colleague doesn't know if you can be trusted, your success is certainly going to be limited. And if you're not consistent, they won't know if they can count on you. Your response and your performance might be fine on one day but shaky the next. Consistency is really the key to success, and it is not being valued as a trait in the current business climate.

The scary part is that consistency isn't that hard to achieve—dogs are great at being consistent. They expect to be walked at the same time every day, don't mind taking the same route, eating the same food, and sleeping on the same blanket every night. Watch your dog go through a typical day sometime, then randomly watch it again. The uncanny repetition of activity, in the same order and at the same time every day, will astound you. This, from a creature who can't tell time and has no idea that one day is different from another.

So if dogs can be consistent, why is it so hard for us humans?

Well, to be fair, our lives are considerably more complicated than a dog's. If all we had to do was find a warm spot to lie in the sun all day, broken up by some eating, some walking, and some taking care of "business," we might achieve a little more reliability than we do now, as well. But in today's split-second society, where communications, decisions, and changes happen in the blink of an eye—and faster—we have a difficult time remembering all the things we intend to be consistent about.

On the other hand, that might be letting us off the hook just a little too easily. Sure, things are happening faster, and there are more things happening in the average day now than ever before (it is estimated that we now receive a greater number of advertising messages in one week than our grandparents did in one year). But isn't all that technology we developed supposed to help us cope with these things? We forgot someone's birthday—what's the matter, we don't have a Palm Pilot? We didn't send a thank-you note for the business dinner last night? Why, doesn't our computer have an e-mail program, even if we don't actually have a stamp and a pen?

There are no honest excuses for being inconsistent, and you can rest assured that if you're not consistent, your competition will be. After all, consistency is simply a policy of doing certain things in the same way every time a certain situation arises. If you always send thank-you notes, you don't have to worry that you didn't send a thank-you note for one important occasion. If you always send birthday cards, there's very little chance you won't send one to the one person who will be deeply hurt if you don't.

Technology, in fact, *can* help you be more consistent. Any computer with access to the Internet can find any number of Web sites that will offer reminders of particular events on the calendar (including birthdays, anniversaries, meeting dates, etc.) for no fee at all. Those who travel outside the office frequently can carry a personal planning unit (Palm Pilot) or a laptop or handheld device that will wirelessly connect to the Internet and access those sites, or keep them in memory to remind you when necessary.

Forgetting is not an excuse.

If you make an effort upon meeting someone to remember her name, and use it throughout the meeting, that can be seen as a charming gesture, and one that may help you ingratiate yourself with that person. But if you go to the next meeting with that same person and obviously forget the name, you undo the good you did and probably do a considerable amount of damage. What is more insulting than being introduced to the same person over and over again? It would make anyone feel insignificant.

You can easily avoid this scenario by making a note of a new person's name immediately after the first meeting, when the memory is still fresh, and then consult the notes from that meeting before entering a second. It's a simple process, one that takes very little time, costs virtually nothing, and can make a very large difference in your relationship with that person and her company. So why not do it?

Lack of preparation is not an excuse.

Some workers, particularly those in lower-level positions, sometimes feel their jobs are menial, that they don't make a difference to the company as a whole. Therefore, they don't necessarily pay as much attention to doing the work efficiently or accurately. Think about the counter help at the local fast-food restaurant. Do they seem to *care* whether the food is actually brought to you quickly? This becomes a scarier proposition when we wonder if the worker on the automotive assembly line or the maintenance crew at the airport is taking a similar mental coffee break.

Even if management is to blame for not inspiring lower-level employees, there is no reason any work in any company should be done sloppily or with indifference or contempt for the end product. There should be no tolerance for substandard work in any field. If an employee has any ambition at all—even if it is not related to this field—he must perform his job with as much attention to detail and to the end product as if he were hopelessly fascinated by the process.

Indifference to the work is absolutely no excuse.

To be consistent, and to be consistently *charming*, a person has to have dedicated a portion of her mind to the task for use all the time. It's not something that can be accessed when needed—charm is a full-time job that never ends. There are no lunch breaks, no vacations, and no retirement plans. It is necessary to change the way your mind works until charm is your first nature. It should never occur to be anything else in all situations.

That's what "consistency" means. It means that you don't miss occasions to be charming because you never stop thinking about being charming. It means that it would never occur to you to insult someone, even unintentionally, because you've made it your business never to do that. It means that you go the extra mile all the time, so that it doesn't feel like doing anything "extra" at all. It is simply what you always do.

That's consistency.

It draws to the forefront the concept of perception versus reality. In the public relations business, in which I work, perception is crucial. It is the public's perception of our clients, their thoughts and feelings about our clients based on observations, that make a difference to us. Because the public at large doesn't get to know celebrities on a one-to-one basis, the *images* that celebrities present and perpetuate is extremely important.

But reality is also vital, and there's a reason for that. Even if you can't know Tom Hanks on a personal basis, and you are simply buying in to the image he decides to project (and I have no reason to think Mr. Hanks isn't as fine a human being as walks this earth—I don't know him personally), don't you think it's easier for Tom to project that image under any circumstances if it's really close to his actual personality? Doesn't it simply make sense that he would more effectively emit that aura if it were who he really is?

Take that and compare it to your own image, the one that you're trying to cultivate and project to your associates, clients, competition, and friends. Yes, you're trying to build up the amount of charm you exhibit, but that doesn't mean you're lying—it's there inside you. You're simply making a more conscious effort to bring out the charm you already have, not creating a false persona that bears no resemblance to your true personality.

Charm is something that everyone has, and only some people *use*. That's the difference. If you put your mind to work on the problem of developing charm, you can do it. (Notice I used the word "developing" and not "creating." You can't just manufacture charm where no raw material exists, but everyone has *some* charm to build on; there are various styles, one for each person.)

You've learned how to develop your own charm, and using your own personality, you can create your own *style* of charm. That means you don't have to follow the same exact rules and do the same exact things as everyone else, even when you're trying to be consistent. You just have to follow your *own* rules and do the same things *you* do all the time, in your own way. If you're a naturally funny person, use your humor as part of your charm (we'll get to that in the next chapter). If you're not, be serious, but in a charming way. You don't have to send everyone a birthday card every year if that's not your style, but if you do, sent it to *everyone* and send it *every year*. That's the lesson of consistency.

As with most things, consistency in charming your way to the top comes down to the concept of thinking about what the other person wants, and choosing to deliver it. And that can start with what *you* want. If you feel touched and honored when someone unexpectedly sends you a birthday card, you should do that for others. If it wouldn't move you at all, don't bother, but come up with something that would make a difference to you and then do that.

Or, make an individual assessment of each person you want to charm (sometimes this has to be done in a split second, when you meet someone new or pass someone on the street), determine what sort of thing that person would find ingratiating, and do that. Remember that it's all about doing unto others as they would have you do unto them. If that happens to fit what you would want done to you, that's all the better.

Consistency is simply the act of doing something on a regular basis, to the point that you no longer have to consciously assess each situation and go through the mental gymnastics of determining what should be done. Repetition will bring about a certain amount of consistency, and the rest is common sense.

Although, it should be noted, that sense is not as common an attribute as we'd like it to be.

~~ Chapter 19 ~~

A Sense of Humor Is Required

This guy walks into a bar—you're gonna love this one . . .

Okay, maybe not. Using humor to increase your charm is not a function of telling jokes. Don't worry—you're not required to be Jerry Seinfeld in order to be thought of as a well-humored person.

Perhaps it would be helpful at the onset to make a distinction between being *humorous* and being *funny*. Yes, in order to be charming, a sense of humor is required. No, you don't have to be a comedian for it to work for you.

A *funny* person is one blessed with the gift of humor above what most of us have when we're born. They are the entertainers at parties and in nightclubs; they are *actively* humorous, drawing attention to their wit intentionally and skillfully. There's no explaining who is a funny person—you know it when you see it, without question.

Being *humorous*, or more to the point, a person with a sense of humor, is a central segment of charm. And because of that, it contains

152

many of the qualities of charm. For example, being a humorous person is mostly about the needs of others, not yourself.

Having a sense of humor is as much about *appreciating* other people's humor as it is about having your own. People like to think they're funny, and if you listen to them and indicate you've found something they've said or done amusing, you are being charming (assuming, of course, that they *intended* to be funny—if they didn't, you're in a bit of a spot).

Sharing a sense of humor is an extremely powerful thing, and it is a huge asset in charming your way to the top. Listening to another person's anecdote about a business or personal matter will indicate your interest in him or her, which is key to developing a charming reputation. And if that story should happen to end in a humorous fashion, your appreciation will cement the bond between you and the person telling the story.

Learning to tell a story yourself is an even greater asset, as it can establish you as a naturally humorous person who is at ease in social and business situations. One piece of advice often given to people about to deliver a speech in public is "open with a joke." You don't have to tell jokes, but knowing where the humor lies in a situation and pointing it out will never hurt.

Self-deprecation

It can help to use *self-deprecating* humor—the kind that is pointed at yourself, rather than others. This is especially effective because it shows you to be modest and self-aware, and to have a sense of humor about your own faults.

Telling jokes or making humorous comments about other people is always a risky proposition. Your listener might be easily offended, might know the person about whom you're speaking (or know someone to whom the comment applies), or might simply find it offensive that you are getting a laugh at someone else's expense.

Making yourself the butt of the joke, on the other hand, is considerably safer, since you are not insulting anyone other than yourself, and the person to whom you're speaking will immediately understand that you are not speaking seriously.

My friend the freelance writer Jeff Cohen is extremely good at using self-deprecating humor as part of his charm. Jeff is a quick wit (his novels showcase his humor beautifully), and often makes jokes at his own expense. He says it's a self-defense mechanism: "I make the joke before someone else can."

Not an especially tall man, Jeff makes jokes about his height frequently. He once told me that he can stand on his toes and reach five foot six "when I want to be intimidating." And when his son, who is fourteen years old, surpassed Jeff in height, Jeff noted that "he's taller than me, which is not an especially difficult thing to do. If he makes it to five foot nine, we're throwing a block party."

Notice that the humor here (and it's funnier when Jeff tells it) is all directed at the speaker himself. He doesn't grouse about tall people taking up all the good spots at the parade or complain about his son now being too tall for him to discipline. It's not someone else's fault—it's Jeff's, and that's what makes the humor *charming*.

People who can make fun of themselves, but avoid making fun of others, are probably those most likely to be described as "charming." They have made a series of choices that demonstrate their commitment to caring about others ahead of themselves, and continue to demonstrate it through constant reinforcement.

Think of it this way. Both Bill Cosby and Don Rickles were headline comedians in the 1960s and beyond. Each had a style that was unique and noticeable: Cosby told stories, chiefly about his childhood, in which he was often the butt of the jokes, never swore, smiled frequently, and always respected his audience. Rickles was a take-no-prisoners insult comic, using the audience as the foil for his barbs, directly assaulting people verbally, generally with the disclaimer that he was kidding, and talked about other celebrities and their foibles rather than his own.

Both were very funny and very successful. But would you consider both of them *charming*? Not really. Cosby had great charm, while Rickles was someone you'd prefer to have talking to someone else, not you. He was a little intimidating and a bit scary. Cosby became so beloved he had at least four hit television shows built around him; Rickles's attempts at television—where the audience has to invite you *into their homes*—were not very successful.

Keep in mind that we're not debating what is or is not funny here—Sam Kinison built a huge reputation in the 1980s as a bold, fiery comedian and was extremely funny, but "charming" was not a word you'd use to describe him, or the onstage persona he developed. People like Seinfeld or Ellen DeGeneres, who might not have been as innovative, but were still funny and also related to the audience in a more ingratiating manner, achieved success equal to or surpassing Kinison's. I would contend it's because their personalities were seen as more *charming* than his, not funnier.

In humor, as in all other aspects of charm, the concept of empathy is important. Keeping the audience's (in whatever situation—the audience can be one person within the sound of your voice) feelings in mind is imperative. If you manage to determine what will amuse someone else and not offend that person, you have a very good chance of being seen as humorous. If you guess wrong, or get caught up in the situation and go too far, you will have fences to mend—and a defensive position is never the most desirable one.

It's not simply a question of not telling ethnic jokes, although those are always in atrocious taste and should be avoided at all costs. Making remarks about any group—women, police officers, short people, gardeners—is guaranteed to be risky, and never recommended, especially when you're talking to people you don't know very well.

More than following that simple rule, the question of *tone* becomes essential. Being jovial and friendly is more important in a business situation than being funny. You can tell hilarious jokes, but if people don't think you're a warm, understanding person, that won't matter much when it comes time for a promotion or a contract.

Humor is a shared experience, one that both parties have to find enjoyable for it to be charming. Comments or jokes that find fault with someone (other than yourself) are best avoided. Remarks about politics, religion, sex, and, in some cases, sports teams can be touchy (people are awfully sensitive about their sports teams!), and should be avoided unless you know your audience's sensibilities very well. *Very* well.

If you don't feel comfortable with humor, and you still want to use it in your conversations with associates or clients, take your time. Perhaps it's best to wait until you have an accurate read on the people you're talking to before you introduce remarks that might be construed more than one way. If you feel *really* uncomfortable with humor, never force it; you should simply become a receptive audience for the humor of the other people involved, and be seen as that, rather than as someone who thinks he's funny and is sadly mistaken.

10 Tips for Using Humor in Business

1. Don't—unless you know the people you're with well
   enough to gauge their threshold of offense.

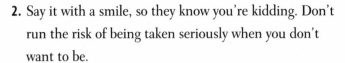

2. Say it with a smile, so they know you're kidding. Don't run the risk of being taken seriously when you don't want to be.

3. Stay away from references to groups of any type, and I mean *any* type.

4. Don't tell jokes—tell stories that relate to the business at hand and may be humorous, or be witty in conversation, if you have a talent for that.

5. Listen to the other person's humor—not only will he find that charming in itself, but it will also give you a feeling for what that person finds funny.

6. Don't attack with humor—you'll come off as petty and mean. Instead, keep things friendly and jovial whenever possible.

7. If there has to be a butt for your jokes—it's your own. Self-deprecating humor is the best for situations in which you don't know the other person extremely well, because it's unlikely someone will object to your making fun of yourself.

8. Never get yourself into a situation in which you're not comfortable with the humor being exhibited. If you're uncomfortable, you won't be humorous, and the chances are, the other people will be just as uncomfortable as you.

9. Know when to quit. Nothing is as irritating as someone who started out funny and ran the joke into the ground. Violence may ensue.

10. It's fun to be seen as funny—but it's more important to be seen as competent and useful. This is business, so make business your top priority. Being funny (if you are)

is just one way of ingratiating yourself to others—it's not
for everyone, and it shouldn't be forced. Keep in mind
that your business is what this is all about.

Some people feel that reciting memorized comedy routines makes
them funny. It's the same as saying that reading the libretto to *La
Traviata* makes one a great singer.

The sad truth is that some people are born funny, and some aren't.
That doesn't mean people who are born without the "funny" gene have
no sense of humor—many of them do, and make the best audiences
for comedy. Some are witty conversationalists or observers of irony.
Others are very good at noticing the amusing aspects of a situation, but
not great at recounting it. That's okay. Use the talents you have to your
advantage, instead of trying to emphasize talents you *don't* have—if
you do that, you'll come across as someone trying much too hard to
amuse. The term "flop sweat" had to start somewhere.

Do an honest assessment of yourself. Are you a person who has a
strong sense of humor? Do your friends comment on your wit, or do
you think you're more an appreciator of humor? Don't try to be something you're not. If you really aren't at all a funny person, there is no
point in trying to be—it will only worsen your situation. Instead, use
the talents you have, and charm people with your great capacity for
appreciating *their* humor. If *they* are not humorous either, set humor
aside and stay focused on the business at hand. Forced humor is far,
far worse than no humor at all.

If nothing else, however, take great pains never to take *yourself* too
seriously. People who don't see the silliness inherent in themselves,
their capacity to do the wrong thing, or to overemphasize a situation,
are worse than bores; they are pompous. They are as far from charming as it is possible to get without actively trying to insult others.

Some people believe it's a sign of weakness to laugh at yourself. They think that if you point out a mistake you might make (and, being human, we all make them), you are showing weakness and losing respect from those involved in the meeting, conversation, or business deal. They are wrong. The ability to see your own flaws, acknowledge them, and have a chuckle at your own expense will only *enhance* the respect you get from others, because they will understand your own self-awareness and your appreciation for other people. Those who think they are flawless or incapable of being seen making a mistake are beyond pompous. They are humorless, imperious people who should not be trusted with major business decisions.

It's not just the ability to use self-deprecating humor I'm talking about—it's a willingness to laugh when someone else points out that your belt missed a loop in your pants, or that your assistant spelled your own name wrong on the contract. Such situations lend themselves to one of two approaches: you can have a chuckle and move on, or you can become exceptionally angry, ream out the person responsible for the mistake (never acknowledging that it could have beeen you), and create a scene that makes everyone in the room uncomfortable.

Which do *you* think is more charming?

Again, here a simple self-assessment, made before a conference or meeting, can be very helpful. Think about the way you usually feel before one of these events. Are you nervous? Confident? Intimidated? Depending on how you normally react, you may be more or less relaxed, and therefore willing to accept a little good-natured teasing or a mistake or two. If you tend to be a little more tightly wound before such an event, it's probably best to look back on the relaxation methods we discussed earlier, or whatever normally works for you, in order to get yourself into a more confident, receptive state of mind.

Remember, much that is charming about humor is based on attitude and relaxation. If you're "loose," your colleagues are likely to be more at ease themselves, and that means your personality—be it a charming listener or a charming talker—will come across more naturally and be received more favorably. Think ahead, and you can succeed more easily.

Humor is subjective. What I think is hilarious you might find sophomoric or simply worthy of a light chuckle. Neither of us is wrong; it's simply a question of taste.

What that means is that you can't be sure of humor when you're starting a business relationship (or any other kind). It's better to hold back initially and assess the situation before trying to overwhelm the conversation. Sometimes, relationships "click" immediately, and you'll know if someone else's sense of humor is similar to yours, or if it's not. But in the case of humor, when in doubt, waiting is the best policy.

All of which reminds me of an old story you'll probably find hilarious. See, this guy walks into a bar . . .

No. Never mind.

Chapter 20

Your Reputation Precedes You

It's true that charm can help you build a reputation that will strengthen relationships and open doors for you. If you are perceived as a charming person, particularly one whose sincerity is beyond reproach, word will get around fast.

Every industry is a small town. Within a business, even competitors talk about the players in the field, and personalities are often discussed. Gossip isn't just a thing for housewives hanging laundry over clotheslines anymore, if it ever really was. Businesspeople discuss each other all the time, and a reputation is something that you can influence, but not control.

All of this is fine if you are just entering your chosen field, and have no previous image to precede you. If you are just beginning your career, or starting work in an industry new to you, the training you've undergone to increase your charm can be a tremendous benefit in building your professional reputation. But what if you're not changing jobs or starting a new career—can charm help you repair a reputation that might not be the best, or will it hurt if you suddenly begin doing things you've never done before?

As they say, I've got good news and bad news. The bad news is that a reputation is a very difficult thing to overhaul entirely—in my years as a Hollywood publicist, I've learned that a personality is much easier to introduce to the public than it is to reintroduce it to the public. Once people believe, whether correctly or not, that they "know" you, it will be an arduous task to change their perception. It can be done, but it's not at all easy.

The good news, though, is that charm can help, and it can't hurt. Even if you're perceived as a hard worker and a serious person, both positive attributes in business, charm can enhance your reputation, assuming you introduce it into your persona gradually, and not try to be everyone's best friend all beginning on a particular Wednesday.

Keep in mind that a reputation is more difficult to change than it is to establish. Working in Hollywood, I've worked with many personalities when they were just beginning, such as Vanna White, Demi Moore, and Michael J. Fox, and while it's never easy to launch a stellar career—or everybody would do it—it is considerably less difficult than changing the public's perception of an entertainer after it is well established. When I worked with Charlton Heston, he was already known as the actor who played Moses, Ben-Hur, and the astronaut in *Planet of the Apes*. Convincing the general public that he was still a relevant actor and not just a resonant baritone voice was trickier; we managed it, but it wasn't a simple task.

Start with the idea that you'd like to *build* a reputation, not just have one immediately. A general perception of your personality is something that others will come to naturally—you can't force it down their throats. You can, certainly, lead them in the direction you'd like them to go, but there are no guarantees that they'll follow.

To begin and develop the reputation you want (as someone who is charming and effective in business), consider a few of the following steps:

- First, your reputation has to be based on truth. People will perceive what is true about you, and report it. So emphasize those qualities you already have that people will consider charming—we've already discussed the vast majority of them.
- That doesn't mean you can't decide which *parts* of the truth you want to emphasize. Obviously, the skills you've learned here already will be at the forefront of your plan—make especially sure you're at your charming best when meeting someone for the first time.
- Avoid trying too overtly to push your own agenda. Don't ask people if they find you charming. Allow the perception to take hold on its own.
- Try to surround yourself with people *you* think are charming. A good percentage of public perception is in association— choose to associate with the type of person you want to be in the public's eye.
- Do public things that are charming—that is, make sure your activities in the public arena, whatever they are, carry with them your version of charm. If you contribute heavily to charity, there's no harm in doing so publicly. If you do something to help the environment in your area (some businesses "adopt" a section of highway, and are responsible for its maintenance), there's no reason it has to be a secret.

ઢ Don't be shy. Publicity is part of most businesses, and there's
no reason your own charm can't be part of every press release
you issue. Use gentle humor; show your modesty even as you
glorify an achievement. Use your well-developed skills, but do
so in a public forum. You're doing publicity anyway—it might
as well include a little charm.

My business is all about reputation, from the inside and the outside.
Not only do I have to consider the reputations of my clients, each of
whom has developed very carefully the face she wants to show the
public (and most often, it's the true face, with only a little makeup),
but each time I place a press release, host a function, or make a phone
call to a newspaper or broadcast media, I'm putting my *own* reputation on the line, as well. Sometimes, the association with famous
names helps, but other times, it does the opposite. A lot depends on
the name being mentioned.

　　If, for example, I'm calling to promote a television actor who is trying to make the jump to feature films, and my news story is about his
being cast in his first leading role, mentioning that name will not be a
detriment to my own reputation. I'm associating myself with someone
on his way up in the entertainment business. And usually, someone in
that position will be careful to put a charming face forward to the
public, so scandal should not be a problem.

　　If I'm dealing with an established personality, the reaction to the
name when I call will obviously be colored by the other person's
opinion of that public personality. If it's a political figure, it's possible
the editor, producer, or reporter might have an opinion that agrees with
or disagrees with my client's position on certain issues. I'm not going
to be able to change her mind on the subject, but maybe I can communicate my client's personality a little more clearly, or simply state

the reason for the call as plainly as possible and treat it as a business situation.

Either way, the entire conversation will be affected by the personality of someone who isn't actually on the phone—the client. And that perception, the preconceived notion of my client's reputation, is either an obstacle or a helpful tool, and I have no control over which it might be.

Sometimes, I know that the client's name will probably solicit a negative reaction. If I'm doing crisis control with a celebrity who has, in the public's mind, done something negative (consider some examples with which I had no connection: the 2003 Michael Jackson scandal, the Phil Spector murder charge, or anything Roseanne ever did), and I want to get the celebrity's point of view (usually some type of explanation or apology) into the public eye, I have to present that case to the media. Often, reporters and their editors or producers will come to me looking for a comment, but in some cases, I have to initiate contact, and I know that not only the member of the press but also the public at large is going to have an opinion on the statement I'm issuing even before they see it.

All I can ask in a situation like that is for the listener to try to approach the topic with an open mind, and in such cases, I have to use as much charm as I can muster. I start by talking to the media members I know personally, make sure I mention some recent occasion where we saw each other, and be absolutely sure to call them by name frequently. I do everything I can to identify myself as a friend, but a friend with a professional agenda, and one that I hope will be accepted in professional terms.

My reputation, then, is the one that's being evaluated. If the reporter I'm speaking to has heard of me, knows me personally, or has heard me mentioned as a publicist who will not mislead the press, I have a decent shot at getting a fair hearing.

If—and I hope this is never the case—the media representative has heard about me from someone who has an ax to grind or simply doesn't like me, he or she might begin with bad information that will not only damage my case in this situation, but could sully my reputation over-all and my dealings with this reporter for quite some time. There's no way of knowing if someone in your business has heard something about you that isn't true, but it's always a danger.

If I don't know the person I'm calling (which is often the situation, since there are thousands of press people and just one me), I have to hope my reputation is a good one or failing that, hope that this person has never heard my name before. In either case, I have to make sure I'm on my best charming behavior during the time we're talking. If my reputation has been badly represented and the reporter has a negative image of me, I might not get to speak to him at all, but if I do, I won't know this is the case. So I have to keep up the charm as strenuously as I can in all encounters with the press, and with other professional contacts.

There's a lesson to be learned in the scenario I presented above. Your reputation isn't necessarily all about *you*. It's also about the people with whom you associate, and the companies with which you are affiliated. Sometimes, your reputation is less your own than that of the organi-zation you represent. You might be a fine, upstanding individual, but if your company's name was just in the newspaper in relation to a huge scandal, your reputation has taken a hit. How many people these days are proud to have the name "Enron" on their résumé?

Obviously, you're not going to choose your associates strictly on the basis of the good or bad they can do your reputation. But it is a con-sideration, and you might consider the "where-there's-smoke-there'sfire" proverb. Sometimes, a bad reputation is well earned, and if you know someone whose overall image is one of deceit and dishonesty, well, this might not be future partner material for you. Naturally, you need to investigate any allegations thoroughly yourself and make your own evaluation—you don't want to be taken in by false information—but a red flag is a red flag. Make sure you do the legwork and find out if any negative rumors you hear about a friend or colleague are true. If you can, help. If you can't, don't get so involved that your own image will be tarnished.

If you discover that a negative rumor about yourself has surfaced, you have to move quickly. In our society, a rumor becomes fact in twenty-four hours if it is not refuted plausibly.

If false information about you or your company is being disseminated within or without your industry, you need to first make sure it *is* false, then immediately make as public a statement as you can to those who might have heard it or been affected by it. Absolutely deny anything you know to be false.

Unfortunately, sometimes negative information turns out to be true. If, through some oversight or miscalculation, you have made a mistake that damages your reputation, do yourself a favor—*don't try to deny it*. Lies are worse than mistakes. Richard Nixon might have managed to remain president if he had immediately taken responsibility for the wrongdoing associated with his campaign, but its cover-up brought him down. Denial, when untrue, will always be discovered, and it will always be damaging. Don't fall into that trap—it's not even close to charming.

Remember: charm is not about lying. Charm isn't about pulling the wool over the eyes of those who trust you. It's about making sure the other person feels you care about him. So own up to your mistakes and tend to your reputation. And when you have to admit to something negative, or defend yourself against an untrue rumor, do so by making it about the other person, and his trust.

Make sure he knows that his trust in you is very important to you, and I don't mean in the way all the phone mail systems try to convince us that our calls are "very important" to the company putting us on hold. Communicate your concern over the betrayal and the shock he must have felt when he became aware of the (true or untrue) rumor. Emphasize how this worries you, how you wouldn't betray his trust for anything, and either deny the untruth or admit the responsibility and apologize for the mistake.

A reputation is a tricky thing—it can take years to build, and change in a split second, for the worse or the better. It can turn on something as monumental as a capital crime, or something as trivial as an elevator door held open a few extra seconds. It can mean the difference between success and failure in business, but it can shift perspective as quickly as a frog's tongue going after a fly.

What's important, from a charming perspective, is the continuing vigilance you exhibit. If you're always on your game, if you're always at least trying to be as charming as you can, you are already miles ahead of most people with whom you compete. But you have to be thinking not just of how to be charming, but about how it's going to look to others—that's what makes a reputation. And you have to make sure you're projecting the positive aspects of your true personality—because the truth is much easier to perpetuate than a lie, and longevity and consistency are what keep a reputation strong.

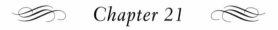

Chapter 21

Telephone Charm

It's not a revelation that we don't act the same on the telephone as we do face-to-face. Everyone can think of a time when he hid his true feelings—perhaps even his true circumstances—when speaking to someone else on the phone. The fact that videophone hasn't really caught on yet supports the point—we don't really *want* people to know exactly what we're doing when we're talking to them on the telephone.

Part of the reason for that feeling is the anonymity telephones offer us. The phone has always been, given its limitations to conveying only sound, a shield to hide behind. Even now, picture phone is an option used sparingly, and never continuously, so the sender can choose which image to communicate. We don't want to surrender our sense of safety from behind the shield of the phone.

Charm, remember, relies on sincerity to be its most effective. False charm is the kind of slimy, slick commodity that immediately repels, rather than attracts. So even when we're not being seen in a conversation, it's best to react as honestly as possible.

Still, in business, our circumstances and our attitudes may not always be the best image to project, even when we are having a significant business conversation. We may look distracted reading over documents or checking our e-mail, even when we are as focused as we can be on the phone conversation. The key is to understand what information is being communicated, and in what way.

In short, there is such a thing as "telephone charm." Surely you've noticed it in others—it is as welcome and unexpected as a bright warm day in February. Most people use the telephone as an instrument of attack, hiding behind the relative anonymity of the situation to forget the rules of civility and common courtesy, and never even approach charm. Often, one can get off the phone with a business associate and feel pummeled or at least disoriented from the abrupt tone and demanding nature of the conversation. When you find someone who truly exercises charm on the phone, a feeling of relief and gratitude can dominate after the conversation is ended. And you can do that for others.

It's not hard to be charming on the telephone; in fact, it's probably easier to be charming when you're relying simply on your voice and don't have to concern yourself with the way you look. Charm is simply the art of convincing other people you care about what concerns them, and all the usual aspects of charm apply on the phone, but they all have to be conveyed by voice.

You don't have to smile on the phone. You don't have to make eye contact or maintain it, and you don't have to concern yourself with your appearance at all. Telephone charm requires a few of the practices you've already learned, with special emphasis on those that are conveyed by sound.

For example, *tone of voice* is going to be very important. If your tone is bored and distracted, no matter how interested you may actually be, the person with whom you're talking is going to have a negative impression of you. You have to monitor your own tone, and keep it engaged and friendly at all times, unless there's a very good reason to present yourself otherwise. Remember, the person you're talking to has no other sensory data to rely upon; she can't see the look in your eye or the wrinkle of concentration on your brow. She can only hear what you are sending across the wire (or airwaves). Make sure you don't misrepresent yourself, especially unintentionally.

Equally important, though, is what you don't say. If *listening* is vital to charm in a face-to-face situation (and it is), it's twice as important on the phone. Make sure the person on the other end of the line understands that what he says is just as important to you as what you say. Do that by allowing space for him to talk, and by responding to what he says with a clear thought, not by anticipating a certain comment and making what seems to be the standard response.

For example, if you ask someone casually, "How are you?" and you expect the standard response, "Oh, fine," you're going to be seen as awfully callous when the other person says, "Actually, I broke my leg last weekend," and you answer, "Great!"

That's not so charming.

There's a charming way to make a business call, and other ways that are not. If, for example, you have an assistant dial the call, then ask for the person you're calling, and put you on the phone last, it may be efficient, but it's not charming. The person you're calling doesn't like having his time deemed less important than yours before the conversation even begins. *Make your own phone calls.*

The modern technology of phone calling has added layers of possible charming—or rude—behavior to the activity. For example, *call waiting* seems like a very useful tool, particularly for small businesses that might not be able to afford multiple phone lines. If a call comes in while you're on the phone, you want to be able to handle the potential client or current client who's on the line, and do so as quickly as possible.

But with that convenience comes a responsibility, both to the incoming caller and the person to whom you're already talking. Now, a choice must be made, and the person on the other end of your phone line knows it. And no matter how kindly you might put it, and no matter how mature and reasonable the other person is, when you choose one call over the other, you run the risk of offending.

The only thing to do in most cases, unfortunately, is to let the new caller hear ring after ring and eventually give up. If the call you're already on is a relatively casual one, you might venture to find out who the new caller is, in case it turns out to be an important business contact. But there's always a danger you'll lose your status as a charmer.

Even more problematic is the *answering machine,* or *voice mail.* Screening calls is an acceptable practice in today's society, which doesn't mean it's the least bit charming. How do you feel when you're in the middle of a message on someone's machine and he picks up, explaining he was screening calls? Do you wonder how often he did the same thing and chose not to take your call? What he might have been doing when that happened?

Sometimes improvements in technology make it harder to be charming. Cary Grant didn't have to deal with wireless phones and voice mail.

The best thing to do, if you're going to have some sort of answering mechanism (and virtually everyone does these days) is never to pick

up the phone in the middle of the incoming message. If you're screening your calls, and someone calls—even someone you want to talk to
right now—simply let the message complete, wait a few minutes, then
call the person back, saying that you "just got in," or were "out for a
moment." Consistency is the most important thing here—if you pick
up even occasionally during a message, your callers will always wonder
what's *really* going on when you don't.

Wireless technology adds another factor to the already-complicated
equation—now, it's almost impossible for someone to be unavailable,
and that makes it more difficult to be charming whenever the phone
rings. There are *some* things that make it difficult to answer the phone,
and we all know what they are.

Some callers are persistent. They're going to try the office phone,
and then the wireless phone if they can't find you in. If you really do
keep everything turned off, and they can't reach you, it might paint you
as something other than the charming, accommodating person you're
trying to be.

On the other hand, there is no reason that even a charming person
has to sacrifice her entire life and all privacy simply to maintain a reputation. That's just too much to ask of anyone.

So how does the charming businessperson walk that tightrope? It's
a balancing act that often takes a good deal of tact and planning to
manage. The key is to make it clear that if you're unreachable, it's not
that you *wanted* to be; it was simply that it couldn't be avoided. Cellu-
lar phones are not allowed to be turned on in doctor's offices; it's
always possible to say you were having a checkup when the call came
through (assuming it's not at 11 p.m., which might seem suspicious).
Calling back with the disclaimer "If I'd known it was *you* . . . " is also

an option, and makes the other person feel important in your eyes. That's a strong use of charm.

Telephone charm is never a simple thing. Even in a casual conversation, remarks can be misconstrued or tone of voice can be missed and ignored. When it becomes clear that a misunderstanding on the phone has undermined your charming reputation, the sad fact is, it's best to reconcile in person.

Of course, the better thing than that would be to avoid the situation before it begins. Pay attention on the phone, just as you would in a face-to-face meeting. That's not always as obvious, or as easy, as it sounds, but it is essential. Paying attention is remarkably important in all aspects of charming your way to the top, and on the phone, it is both more difficult and more central. It's easy to be distracted—you don't have the other person to look at, either, and there are often things in the room with you (particularly if you're in your office) that require your attention. Focusing solely on the conversation is not as natural a thing as it is with a flesh-and-blood human in front of you.

When you are the person being called, make sure of your tone before answering the phone. That doesn't mean you have to "rehearse" your greeting, but don't let the situation that's going on before the phone rang influence your demeanor—remember, the person calling you has no idea you just stubbed your toe on your desk or heard a hilarious joke from your coworker, and he or she doesn't want to feel like an intrusion or worse, an annoyance.

Most people's phone demeanors are pretty coarse. We expect that everyone who calls us has been with us all day, knows exactly what kind of day we're having, and should be sensitive to our needs. On the contrary, if someone is taking the time to seek us out on the phone, we should be especially glad to appeal to *their* needs, and put our own on the back burner for a few minutes while we listen carefully to the reason for the call.

The problem is that we are caught up in our own lives, as is only natural. We have a hard time putting the immediate situation in our lives on hold to cater to a ringing phone. Occasionally, when we're not in control, we let that feeling slip into our voices on the phone. It is the worst kind of anti-charm. The message being put out is *why did you bother me now?*

Empathy will once again rule the day. Think how you feel when you call a business associate, particularly one you don't know well. How do you want to be received, especially if you're offering to buy a product or service from this person? Obviously, you'll expect a certain degree of welcome, as well you should. Turn the tables on yourself, and consider the person calling you and how he will feel if you bark at him or sound bored when you answer the phone.

Telephone charm isn't all that different from face-to-face charm, but it does require a different set of skills used in the forefront. It requires greater concentration, because the other person in the conversation exists in a separate place. You must focus on imagining that person in her office, form a picture in your mind, and consider her expectations and hopes for this conversation. Then fulfill them to the best of your ability. That's what charm is all about.

Keep in mind that the telephone is an imperfect instrument—it doesn't really communicate the way two people in the same room can, and it won't even when full-motion video phone is in every home and office. It will always come in second to a face-to-face conversation, for many good reasons. But given the necessities of modern business and the technology available, it's the best possible alternative to a true meeting.

As you charm your way to the top, you'll encounter any number of situations more elaborate and foreign than a simple telephone conversation, but none quite as subtle and taken for granted. Since we all grew up with phones, even wireless phones, we don't think very carefully about the concentration and thought necessary in using them skillfully.

Other forms of technology, newer and more expansive ones, are just as tricky, but we think about them harder because we aren't as comfortable with them, even if we've been using them for years. The telephone's function hasn't changed all that much since the rotary desktop model on our grandparents' end table. But we have to look at it in a new and more thoughtful way if we are going to use the telephone as an instrument of charm.

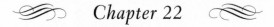 *Chapter 22*

E-charm

If telephone charm seems complex, consider that the technology involved is as familiar as a chair. We've all grown up knowing what a telephone is, how it works, and what it can do. The adaptation of using that technology to convey charm is strictly a question of implementing tactics that would be considered charming with or without the instrument in hand. It's more a question of concentration than anything else.

With more advanced technology, such as computer communication, wireless communication, e-mail, and online chat, the whole process is not quite as familiar, even for those young enough to not remember what a home without a computer looked like. E-charm is a more complex beast, because it combines newer forms of communication with different rules and an overall change in the basic understanding of how human interaction is conducted.

Does that seem daunting? It shouldn't, now that you've come this far. You know how to use your charm. Using it online isn't all that different from face-to-face confrontations or the telephone. Yes, there are some special circumstances to pay attention to, and you do need a little training before you begin, but the basic skills you've learned beginning on page one remain the same.

With the rise of the Internet in the 1990s, an entire culture was born that had never existed anywhere before. Communication between people, groups, and companies on any section of the globe was now possible immediately, and the opportunities truly did seem endless.

Now, with a little more perspective, the Net's flaws are a touch more noticeable, and the magic is becoming perhaps a bit too familiar to be truly astonishing, but the advantages and the possibilities remain, and they are to be cherished.

Think about how you felt when you started using the Internet regularly. The wide oceans of information available at the stroke of a key! The incredible access to virtually every other person on the planet! The ability to promote yourself and your business all around the world—for free (well, almost)!

All that is still part of online life. And it is all possible if you know how to use the Internet and how to avoid the pitfalls we've all found over the years. The Net, after all, is about communication, and in that, one element can help smooth the bumpy spots easier than anything else: charm.

Yes, it's just as important to be charming online as it is in non-virtual life. Those who use the Internet's relative shield of anonymity to vent their rudest and least charming impulses are simply mis-informed or worse—hiding behind a false identity to begin with is something of a problem, and doing so in order to be coarse and mean is simple cowardice. Nothing else.

A "presence" online can mean a good number of things these days. It can be your own personal or professional Web site, the identity (screen name) you use in Internet chat rooms, listserv posts, and bulletin boards. It can be the text messages you send via your wireless phone. It can mean anything that you decide it means as you navigate your way around the World Wide Web (and elsewhere), but it is always a reflection of you. You are still responsible for anything you say, do, or write online. Just as you are responsible to pay for anything you buy at Amazon.com, despite having never entered a store to purchase the product.

It's easy to sit alone behind a keyboard and type words. The hard part is taking responsibility for the words you type. Once you hit the send key, you have committed to those words, put your name on them, and told other people that they reflect your thoughts. Think hard before you hit that key.

It seems more difficult these days for people to take responsibility for their actions—everything seems to be someone else's fault. If you spill hot coffee on yourself at the drive-through, it's the fast-food chain's fault because it shouldn't make its coffee so hot. If your children are getting poor grades in school, it's because the teacher doesn't like them. If your candidate loses the election, it's not because you didn't see a reason to participate in the election or even to vote, it's because the other candidate ran misleading advertising.

Online, it's that much easier to duck responsibility. You don't even have to use your real name (in fact, it's rarely expected, or encouraged) in chat rooms or on bulletin boards. Even when people *know* who you are, when you're sending text messages to colleagues or e-mailing friends, it's always possible to "talk" in such a rushed fashion that no one could possibly blame you for being imprecise. Right?

Well, no. People see printed words, even printed on the text screen of a wireless phone or PDA, as more "official" than spoken ones. Very few oral contracts are still recognized as legal and conversations between two people are often considered "off the record," but written communication, no matter how casual or spontaneous it may be, is considered more serious and binding. It's harder to "take back" something you say when it's there in black and white for everyone to see. Especially since these days, it can be printed out or distributed via e-mail in a matter of seconds.

So statements made in print—any form of print—need to be more, not less, considered than simple spoken statements. It's not that you don't have to mean what you say in conversation—you do— but it will be much easier to call you on statements you make on paper or screen, even when you think you're at your most casual.

E-charm is all about conveying your personality electronically, which is not the same as any other form of communication. Where the telephone took away the senses of touch and sight that are part of a face-to-face conversation, online chat and posts remove even more of the experience. There is no tone of voice to convey the intended meaning of words. There is no emphasis on certain words, no way to chuckle as you say something, so as to indicate you're kidding. Now, your words are being judged strictly on face value—without the face.

Now, it's true that all forms of electronic communication have developed various ways to compensate for these deficiencies—some of them more effectively than others. Posters who read bulletin boards or participate in chat rooms know, for example, that certain "emoticons" are meant to say "just kidding" or "I'm sorry." (Emoticons are a series of symbols meant to convey the look of a smile or a frown or many other expressions. For example, ;-) denotes a wink.) But these are symbols that convey meaning *after* the words have been typed, not along with them, and that's not nearly as effective. If a person feels offended by your statement, even for a split second before seeing the "I'm kidding" signal, even if she shrugs it off, there might be a lingering sense that you said something offensive, or worse, that you blatantly fooled her and then pointed it out, which is not considered charming.

Because online communication is instantaneous, thinking beforehand is geometrically more important. This is no place for "impulse talking," because your words are going to be in plain sight and out of your control in less than one second. You have no recourse, no chance to take things back, no second chances here. Enter a chat room at your own risk, and always take a moment to think before you hit that send key.

Once online, however, there are rules you can follow that might help avoid awkward situations and impulsive, unchangeable mistakes. Most people who are at all practiced in chat rooms will know, for example, not to type their entire messages in capital letters (this is considered "shouting," and is undeniably rude) or to scroll messages vertically, one letter at a time (which goes beyond rude, into the territory of "obnoxious" and can sometimes result in expulsion).

To go beyond simply not insulting people and continue on until you are charming them, more effort is necessary. As usual, the best plan is to adapt the established rules of charming your way to the top to the situation, in this case, electronic communication across computer screens.

For example, start with the basic principle. Charm is convincing the other people you care about them. This is not as easy online as it is in other situations, but it's far from impossible. You aren't expected to send a warm smile, a comforting tone of voice, and a firm handshake across your modem, but it is possible to convey the same message of interest in the other person's point of view and concern for his goals.

Each chat room, bulletin board, or listserv is dedicated to one interest or another, and you wouldn't be entering this particular area of the Internet if you didn't share that interest, at least to some degree. So you already have a common topic of conversation with everyone else present when you enter for the first time. That's an opportunity to be charming, but a dangerous temptation to be obnoxious, showing off your knowledge rather than letting others discuss and make their own points.

Here, of course, is where the concept of *listening* once again rears its not-so-ugly head. In a conversation, your charm may lead you to long periods of listening and trying to understand your partner's point of view. Online, it's actually easier to listen (despite the fact that nothing is being said aloud), because you aren't responsible in a group situation to fill any uncomfortable silences, particularly since those almost never exist. You need only respond to questions or comments directed specifically at you, and in those cases, again, you should think carefully before responding.

Listening online is a matter of processing the comments being made (which can be quite a task, as in larger chat rooms, comments are made extremely rapidly) and then responding in the charming manner with which you have become familiar, and with which you are now associated. Say the same thing you'd say if the other person or people were in the room with you, but take the time to say it properly, and accurately. Again, no "do-overs" here.

Charming E-mail

Since so much business correspondence these days is done via e-mail, the art of being charming in your e-mail is more important than even just a few years ago. As with most things, this means that the rules are the same for e-mail as they would be for the traditional means of communication, like notes or phone calls. But because of the immediacy of electronic communication, the rules have to be considered more seriously, and the responses must be much, much faster. Consider it letter writing, literally, on speed.

I try as hard as possible to answer every phone call that comes into my office the same day. No exceptions and no excuses, my office answers that call the same day. With e-mail, the rapidity involved has to be increased. This is faster, less formal, and usually, considered more urgent.

In order to be considered charming, I try to answer each e-mail I get as soon as I possibly can, and if I can answer it immediately, I do so. The majority is answered within the hour. That's just common sense, as speed is what e-mail was invented to provide.

But speed is just the beginning with e-mail. Think of how much more sophisticated you are in terms of your e-mail experience than you were when you started. There is a vocabulary, a set of customs and expectations that exists now and didn't exist then. You know what you're in for with e-mail, and you should have a very good idea of what people expect of you when you e-mail with them.

In 1980, Spam was either, depending on your age and sensibility, a lunch option or a Monty Python punch line. Almost no one thinks of it in either of those terms first anymore—spam is the kind of e-mail that causes us to gnash our teeth, hide our screens from our children, and spend money on programs that are supposed to rid us of these nuisances.

To say the least, sending someone spam is not charming. Make sure that anytime you send e-mail out to a list of recipients, the addresses of all the list members are hidden from all the others. Spam is often sent to addresses discovered this way, and making sure—before being asked—that your friends and associates will not be burdened with more unwanted e-mail through their association with you is the definition of thinking about someone else first. And that is charm.

Make sure, also, that *your* e-mail is not seen as spam. If someone wants to stop receiving your e-mail promotional announcements and information, make sure it's easy for them to opt out, and make sure that those who have opted out are, indeed, no longer receiving the information they asked not to get.

Through my business, I send out a daily news service e-mail, *Levine Breaking News*. It is sent to more than 70,000 influencers— an elite list of recipients that includes people in the entertainment industry, politics, publishing, and many other fields. I try to fill it with as much strong information and thought-provoking discourse as possible, and I think it's a very strong addition to anyone's in-box.

But if someone asks me to remove his or her name from the list, it is removed as quickly as I can do it. That's simple courtesy, and it is considered charming.

E-charm doesn't require a new set of skills or a very radical re-thinking of the rules of charm. It does require faster reflexes and some thought, which is not a bad combination in any situation. Charm in the electronic environment is a very large part of today's business climate. If you want to be considered a charming person (and by now, I think you should be convinced that is a very important goal, indeed), in today's society, you need to be thought of as charming in an online environment, because that is where so much of our lives now exist.

So get on that screen, and start charming!

Chapter 23

You Charming Devil, You

You have come a very long way. Beginning without even a definition of charm, you have progressed to the point where you can not only define, but refine the concept of charm in yourself. You can spot it in other people, understand how they are using it, and apply that to your own situations. You can extrapolate the idea of charm to every aspect of your life, determining whether or not you are maximizing the amount of charm you're using at every given moment. Are you being as charming as you can possibly be? You probably know.

Take a deep breath and think about it. You are now charming.

No, really. You are. You've done the work and you've put in the time. You have practiced and planned, emphasized the charming aspects of your personality and brought out some you didn't know you had. You have noted what other people do that especially impresses you, and you haven't so much copied it as adapted it to fit your own needs. You've repeated the same types of scenarios and behaviors

185

enough times that they've become second nature—maybe even first nature. You have used your will and your intelligence and you have learned to be the kind of person you want other people to think you are. You know how to think of the other person first while keeping your own interests at heart.

You are charming.

Bask in that knowledge for a moment, because it is an accomplishment you should be quite proud of. Where others might come to a trait naturally and learn over time how to use it instinctively, you have identified a need in your personality and have made a special effort to fill it. That takes a good deal more determination, more hard work, and more intellect—and you should indeed be pleased with the work you've done and the results you've achieved.

There's just one more thing—you've got to go out and use it.

Yes, you know all you need to know and you have examined the various situations in which your charm will help you. You may even have plotted a course for your career that now includes the element of charm. The hard work and analysis that go into developing charm are behind you. But you still have to put the talent you've developed to work for you, and that means getting out into a real situation and watching your charm kick into gear.

It's not hard, and you already know that from practice and observation. It won't be a major test of your abilities, since you're already confident in the charm you've developed. But there's something about getting out there the first few times and working a room, or charming a potential client on your own, that seems daunting and just a little scary.

There's no need for panic (in fact, there is rarely a need for panic in life—panic doesn't really help anyone very much), and there's no reason to feel unprepared. The work we've done together in this book and the work you've done on your own in your observations and practice are all meant to bolster your confidence. You've done all this before, and you've seen it work. It's simply a question now of putting it into practice and not stopping.

After you finish reading this chapter, make a phone call. Use your phone charm to set up a meeting with an associate, client, or potential client. Make sure you present the opportunity as something that the *other* person will find beneficial, not something you need to do.

When you arrive for the meeting (or when the other person arrives at your home or office, depending on the arrangements that have been made), put the other person at ease by smiling, offering a hand, making a self-deprecating remark. In other words, use your charm. Exercise it. Flex it. You'll notice the difference in the other people in the room.

Of course, between the phone call and the meeting, you'll be practicing your charm in the street, smiling at passersby, at the dry cleaner, in restaurants, and at the gas station. You've been doing this all the time anyway, and it has become a way of life for you. That helps build confidence and shows you that your skills are indeed sharp and working well.

The hard part is making the commitment, deciding that *this* is when you're going to begin. Because you know from reading these pages that once you begin showing the world the charm you've developed, you can't stop, ever. What you don't know is that it will continue to become easier and easier until you barely even notice you're doing it anymore.

Some people *never* start the process of charming your way to the top, and they end up, invariably, on the Charming Hall of Shame:

The Charming Hall of Shame (in no particular order)

1. **Roseanne (Barr, Arnold, or just plain).** From her crotch-grabbing antics on the ball field to her public and cringe-inducing

marriage to Tom Arnold, the former stand-up comedian whose self-named sitcom defined the genre in the 1980s did everything *but* charm her way to the top. She reached the top (as did many on this list) through her undeniable talent, then accepted her fame and fortune as a license to unleash any public behavior that moved her at the moment. The fall was sudden and steep, and to date, Roseanne's career is nowhere near the model it might have seemed at its height.

2. **Michael Jackson.** Forget the allegations and the criminal charges. Forget the plastic surgery (if you can). Forget the bizarre lifestyle and the strange marriages. The act of dangling a baby over a fourth-floor railing merits inclusion on this list all by itself. If you can't think of the needs of an infant ahead of your own, what does that say about your character? (Never mind your charm.)

3. **Joan Collins.** I worked with both Ms. Collins and Linda Evans at the time of *Dynasty*. I've been clear in previous chapters about how charming and gracious Ms. Evans was and continues to be. Let's suffice it to say that the polar opposite of Ms. Evans may be Ms. Collins, and that their characters on that prototypical nighttime soap opera may be indicative of the way they act offscreen, as well.

4. **Charlton Heston.** There was a time when I was honored to work with Mr. Heston, an Academy Award-winning actor who had become something of an icon, practically destined for carving on Mount Rushmore. But with his obsessive identification with some of the extreme elements of the National Rifle Association and his proclamation of "from my cold, dead hands!" Mr. Heston, in my opinion, stained his impeccable reputation significantly and undid much of the charming work he had

done on his personality in the past. His legacy now is partially tainted, and that is sad and unfortunate.

5. **Tommy Lee and Pamela Anderson.** Doing their best to live the heavy-metal lifestyle, this couple went as far as they could, and then considerably farther. When a videotape of the two having sex surfaced on the Internet, and then they started sniping at each other in the press, their divorce became inevitable and ugly to watch; there was no point in doing all that in public. By the time she was blaming him for giving her hepatitis, and he was saying she was overstating the case, it had gone much, much too far.

6. **Burt Reynolds and Loni Anderson.** See above, minus the tape on the Internet. Their divorce hurt both their careers and was far, far too public. Subsequent attempts to revive their careers have met with various degrees of success, but neither has ever reached the heights they had risen to before their marital troubles became a public circus.

7. **Sean Penn.** Yes, he is a gifted, talented, brilliant actor. There is no question of that. But the actor's insistence on brawling with anyone he thinks is invading his "privacy" begs the question: Did someone ask you to become a famous movie star, or was it a decision you made on your own? Did you not realize that "famous" means people will recognize you in public? Take your picture? Ask for an autograph? You don't get to accept the part of the deal you want and reject the rest. Any celebrity who growls at autograph seekers should answer the same questions.

8. **George Steinbrenner.** The owner of the New York Yankees is a distinguished businessman and unquestionably dedicated to putting a winning team on the field for the benefit of the

city's fans (and, it could be argued, his own ego). And don't make any mistake. When he is wooing the latest free agent on the market, he can be an extremely charming man. But Steinbrenner's charm, it has been widely reported, is limited to those he wants something from. Those who work for him are used to being berated, screamed at, and threatened, often for things out of their control or for decisions the "Boss" himself made. When he announced, in the middle of one winter, that the $180 million he was spending on players might force him to drop the dental plan the Yankees were paying for their office staff, charm was nowhere to be seen.

9. **Eminem.** His talent is not in question. And, sometimes, artists have to push the envelope of subject matter to open up discussion in the general public. But glorifying violence against women (or men, for that matter), using racial slurs, and generally trying to shock for shock's sake crosses the line. Art may be art, and it might be relevant, but that doesn't make it charming.

10. **Dennis Rodman.** Compare him to Michael Jordan. Is there really a comparison? A vastly talented player, Rodman eventually became persona non grata in the NBA because teams could no longer put up with his antics off the court. Outrageous, entertaining even, certainly, but charming? Nope, can't make that case.

This is not a list you want to join, unless your particular abilities are so great that you think you can bypass charm and simply overwhelm the world into elevating you to the top of the list. Since an extremely small portion of the general population might fall into *that* category, perhaps it's best to concentrate on using the charm you've worked so hard to develop and cultivate.

After the first meeting you attend at which you start to use your skills, you should evaluate your performance. Did you do what you set out to do? Did the others at the meeting respond the way you expected them to? And most important, did it seem labored to use your charm, or, after all this practice, did the charm flow naturally?

In all likelihood, the answers to those questions (if you answer them honestly) will point to one conclusion you can't avoid: the charm you've worked on has helped you succeed just a little bit more, a little bit more easily, than you might have otherwise. It impressed the people you wanted to impress, and maybe even impressed some people you hadn't considered impressing before you began.

Your charm can then be allowed to grow. You can set up other meetings, continue to practice in every daily situation, and continue to observe the effect charm has on the people in your orbit.

Remember, as we've noted before, this is a continuing, twenty-four hour process that doesn't clock out at the end of the day. But the good news is that the more you use it, the less you have to work at using it.

You have become a charming person, and you've done it by design. That's not cold calculation or manipulation of others, it's the opposite of those. Think about it. You have devoted yourself to thinking about other people's interests even while you think of your own, and you believe that while adopting this practice will help you personally, it's also the right thing to do. Without applying for sainthood, isn't that a pretty altruistic attitude?

Charm is, in the final analysis, something that benefits everyone. It is a pleasure to be around, and often works to the benefit of those being charmed. It also has, as we have noted throughout, many benefits to the person who practices it. But charming your way to the top isn't only about you. It's also about the people you will help and charm along the way.

They won't feel that you've cruelly manipulated them, unless you do. They will believe—and they'll be right—that you are a person who helped *them* along the way and were pleasant to deal with. There really is no problem with that.

Charm is a quality that is easy to spot and difficult to define in most everyday situations. People don't wave a flag over their heads or flash neon signs that say, "I'm using charm," and often those who are the beneficiaries of charm wouldn't even identify themselves that way. It's not supposed to be the most noticeable thing that happens in the course of a day.

For most people you charm, the experience will simply be identified as a feeling that's left over when the meeting, the conversation, or the business deal is completed. And it will be a positive feeling, one that makes them want to deal with you again.

That's why you have to get out there and start using your charm. What are you waiting for?

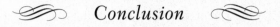 *Conclusion*

View from the Top

Throughout this book, I have tried to impress upon you the importance of charm in the process of ascending the ladder in any business. I believe the case has been well made that charm can make the climb easier and faster, and that it will be a more pleasant experience for everyone encountered along the way, even you.

Once you reach the top of your profession, you might want to look back and think of where you've come, and what has helped you get here from there. Consider the people you've met along the way—were they helped or hurt by your success, and did you use your charm to help yourself, help them, or both?

Charm, we have seen, is a tool, a weapon, and a crutch. It can certainly be a source of inspiration and comfort when needed. It should definitely be the beginning of many warm feelings, as well: gratitude, friendship, allegiance, reciprocation. Those who feel you have done them well will be more inclined to do well by you. Charm develops bonds between and among people, and sometimes, that is even stronger and more important than the success and professional advancement it helps to develop.

The view from the top is one that can be gratifying and terrifying at the same time. It is not wrong to revel in the success you have achieved. It would be a mistake not to think about the things that helped make it possible—like charm. But at the same time, it seems so easy when at the top to fall back down. One stumble, it seems, could land you right back where you started.

Sometimes, that is true. Business is not always a warm, fuzzy activity. Cutthroat competition, rivals from within, and just plain changing market conditions (in any market) can certainly contribute to a downfall—but consider the truly spectacular falls from grace we have seen over the past few years. Businesspeople who had every reason to feel they had accomplished all they had set out to do, who were living lives that many others envied, felt it wasn't enough. They looked for more in terms of monetary and material achievement, and what they ended up with, in many cases, were collapsed careers, toppled corporations, and sometimes, prison terms.

When *you* look down from the top, consider how completely without charm greed is. There is no way to paint a charming face on the concept of always wanting more, even when it is no longer a question of needing, or even wanting, more for any reason other than to have more.

That is not charming. Greed is not charming. It may be a motivational factor for some, but it will never benefit them, because they can't possibly make it seem that their own greed will benefit others, and *that* is how true alliances are made. If charm is the art of convincing others that you care about them, greed is clearly a way of showing others that you don't care about anything other than yourself.

You have other, better, motivators. Yes, you want to make it to the top of your industry, and you are using charm to get there. But in choosing charm over brutal, cold ambition, you are demonstrating something that greed will never be able to provide: concern for something outside yourself. And that will in turn become something that greed can't guarantee in any way—longevity.

It's fine to charm your way to the top. But once you get there, the hard part is *staying* at the top. Charm is even more valuable in this case, because the people who will support you in your career are already in place; they already trust you. They will help because they know your goals include them. Their interests are part of yours. And that will make it easier *not* to plummet from the dizzy height you have achieved for yourself.

You have chosen to charm your way to the top because it makes sense to do so, but also because there is something in your personality that makes it appealing to you. You picked up this book initially because the idea of *Charming Your Way to the Top* was interesting to you—if the title had been *Backstabbing Your Way to the Top*, you might not have had the same impulse, and you certainly wouldn't have read this far into the book.

So don't worry about the view from the top. You'll get to see it, and you'll enjoy it for a good, long time. Because you have chosen to get there with charm, when you could have chosen other ways.

Keep in mind that charm is a life choice, not an activity that can be switched on and off at will. In order to be exercised effectively, charm must be an impulse, an instinct, something that happens without thinking. Just by reading this book, you have not achieved lifelong charm. By practicing the exercises discussed herein, and by making them your nature, you certainly can.

One of these days, when I'm walking down a crowded street in Los Angeles, London, New York, or Chicago, and I'm looking into the eyes of the people who pass me by, perhaps you will be coming in the other direction. If you are, our eyes will certainly meet, since you will be looking into the eyes of all who pass you, as well.

Perhaps at that moment, you will smile in my direction, without considering it, just as you pass on your way to a very busy day. And when you do, I will recognize your charm and your effort to be charming, which will be evident to all those who come into your orbit.

At that moment, I will be very proud. So in advance of that moment, let me thank you for it, since I may not have the time when we pass. Thank you for learning the lessons in this book and for feeling they are important enough to take to heart and make part of your lifestyle. I'm glad the words I put down on these pages made enough of a difference to you that you would make that effort. I'm glad you found the words worthy of your attention and your thought. Thank you for all that.

I'd send you a note, but I don't have your address.

Michael Levine
Los Angeles, California
www.lcoonline.com

Index